Great Houses

of

Mississippi

Great Houses

of

Mississippi

TEXT BY MARY CAROL MILLER

PHOTOGRAPHS BY MARY ROSE CARTER

UNIVERSITY PRESS OF MISSISSIPPI / JACKSON

A Mary Jayne G. Whittington
Book in the Arts

www.upress.state.ms.us

Designed by Todd Lape

The University Press of Mississippi is a member of the
Association of American University Presses.

Frontis: Rosalie, Natchez, Mississippi

12 11 10 09 08 07 06 05 04   4 3 2 1
∞
Library of Congress Cataloging-in-Publication Data

Miller, Mary Carol.
 Great houses of Mississippi / text by Mary Carol Miller ; photographs by
Mary Rose Carter.
  p. cm.
 ISBN 1-57806-674-3 (cloth : alk. paper)
 1. Historic buildings—Mississippi. 2. Dwellings—Mississippi. 3. Historic
buildings—Mississippi—Pictorial works. 4. Dwellings—Mississippi—
Pictorial works. 5. Mississippi—History, Local. 6. Architecture,
Domestic—Mississippi. I Carter, Mary Rose. II. Title.

F342.M55 2004
976.2—dc22   2003026771

British Library Cataloging-in-Publication Data available

This book is dedicated to our parents:

Sara Evans Criss
William Russell Criss

Georgia Robertson Abernethy
Lynn Dunlap Abernethy, M.D.

Contents

Preface   ix

Acknowledgments   xi

Introduction   xiii

FEDERAL STYLE   1

GREEK REVIVAL   23

Cold Spring   4

Auburn   7

Rosemont   11

Rosalie   14

Feltus-Catchings House   17

Lewis House   19

Martha Vick House   27

Magnolia Hill   29

Cedar Grove   31

Wilson-Gilruth House   34

Rowan Oak   37

Melrose   40

Beauvoir   44

The Magnolias   48

Riverview   50

Tullis-Toledano Manor   54

Athenia   57

Strawberry Plains   61

Belmont   64

Mosby Home   68

Dunleith   70

Neilson-Culley-Lewis House   73

Stanton Hall   76

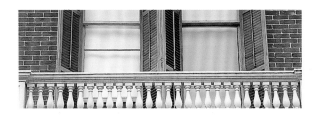

ITALIANATE   81

Rosedale   83

Wohlden   86

Boddie Mansion   90

Ammadelle   93

Mount Holly   97

GOTHIC REVIVAL   101

Manship House   102

Cedarhurst   107

Airliewood   113

ECLECTIC   119

Waverley   120

White Arches   125

Walter Place   127

Longwood   134

Notes   143

Bibliography   145

Index   147

Preface

Every surviving antebellum house in Mississippi is, by virtue of its longevity and endurance, a "great house." Some are physically imposing, such as Dunleith, Riverview, and Waverley, while others are more modest and unassuming, such as Rosemont, the Martha Vick House, and Magnolia Hill. Within the walls of some, history played itself out in dramatic fashion. Ammadelle barely survived fire set by marauding Union soldiers. Cedar Grove still has a cannonball imbedded in the plaster of the parlor. Auburn bore witness to one man's struggle to right a long-standing system of bondage. And the Boddie Mansion gave birth to a college that would celebrate the end of that system. Other houses have no connections to epochal events but have just quietly sheltered generations of the same family, serving more as homes than historic sites.

Size, architectural elegance, and historical significance were considerations in choosing the thirty-five houses that you will meet in this book, but they were not the only factors. We had literally hundreds of sites to choose from, as Mississippi is blessed with an overwhelming abundance of truly outstanding antebellum architecture, from the early Federal style through the dominant Greek Revival examples and including the less common Italianate, Gothic, and Eclectic buildings. We have tried to include representative samples of each of those architectural periods and highlight the landmark houses that define the state's image. But we have also chosen a variety of houses that won't make most books on historic architecture. All are visually stunning in their own way. Many have fascinating stories behind their construction or restoration or salvation. Each is cherished by the people who know it best, those who provide time, countless dollars, and backbreaking (and occasionally heartbreaking) labor and love to keep it standing for the rest of us.

This is by no means a comprehensive review of Mississippi's historic architecture. It's merely an introduction to a representative group of "great houses," each worthy of reverence and preservation. Even casual students of old houses will recognize Dunleith and Waverley and Stanton Hall, but they may wonder why they've never come across Belmont or Strawberry Plains or the Wilson-Gilruth House. In every community, in every corner of Mississippi, there are equally significant houses, many desperate for attention and renovation. They may not all have the towering columns of Dunleith, the history behind the Manship House, or the drama of Waverley's restoration, but they are part of our common heritage and deserving of attention. Our goal in choosing these thirty-five "great houses" is to remind us all of our obligation to protect the best of our past for future generations.

Acknowledgments

We have had the honor and the privilege, over the past year, of photographing and researching thirty-five of the most exceptional houses in Mississippi. Many are still private homes, and we are very grateful to the owners who shared their stories and their time with us. Others are now museums or are owned by preservation groups, and it is always inspiring to see the hard work and dedication which so many professionals and volunteers bestow on our "great houses." We are deeply indebted to all who rearranged their schedules or rushed up a paint job or just made us feel at home.

Thanks go also to the staff at the Mississippi Department of Archives and History for all their help in exploring the histories of these homes. The Historic Preservation Division and the archives library are invaluable in documenting Mississippi's architectural past, and we wish them well in their new quarters, the William F. Winter Archives and History Building.

Joe and Dottie Donaldson's hospitality has been more helpful than they will ever know, and we appreciate their graciousness.

And, as always, our gratitude to our families is foremost. Our schedules (or lack of such) affect theirs, and they are unfailingly patient with us in these book ventures. To our husbands, Jimmy and Michael; our children, Emily and Jim, Claire and Hal, Walker and Janet; and to Sara Criss and Lucy Carter for their encouragement, we extend our thanks.

And very special appreciation is owed to Jerome Lee, who didn't call the Wilkinson County sheriff on us. Keep up the good work at Rosemont.

Following is a list of those who have helped us with this book in one way or another. It couldn't have been done without them.

AIRLIEWOOD: Barbara Fant, Joe Overstreet
AMMADELLE: Dorothy Lee Tatum
ATHENIA: Ben Martin, Barbara Fant, Patricia Evans
AUBURN: Kay Nunn
BEAUVOIR: Patrick Hotard, Jennifer Myers
BELMONT: Fernando Cuquet, John Dean, Jr.
BODDIE MANSION: Beverly Hogan, Kelle Menogan

CANTON: Jim Lacey, Jr.
CEDAR GROVE: Ted Mackey
CEDARHURST: Fred and Linda Belk
COLD SPRING: Jimmie and Mary Katherine Randall
COLUMBUS: Sam Kaye
DUNLEITH: John Holyoke, Mike Worley
FELTUS-CATCHINGS HOUSE: Alex and Ann Ventress
HOLLY SPRINGS: Chesley Thorne Smith, Hubert McAlexander, Milton Winter
LEWIS HOUSE: Holmes Sturgeon
LONGWOOD: Sis Stowers
MAGNOLIA HILL: Michael Wheelis
THE MAGNOLIAS: Jim Crosby, Sara Weillman
MANSHIP HOUSE: Marilynn Jones
MELROSE: Kathleen Jenkins
MISSISSIPPI DEPARTMENT OF ARCHIVES AND HISTORY: Richard Cawthon, Todd Sanders, Clinton Bagley
MOSBY HOME: Bill Mosby

Introduction

In an isolated corner of Mississippi, west of Woodville and south of Natchez, is a quiet and forgotten land of deep gullies, lush foliage, and a scattering of fine old houses. Cold Spring is likely the very oldest, its territorial origins evident in the cantilevered roofline, unadorned Tuscan columns, and interior devoid of decoration. When Dr. John Carmichael sank his roots here and built the mansion, he could have had no idea that his home would be just one of the first of many in a remarkable sixty-year run of architectural exuberance.

Thirty miles north of the sunken road that leads to Cold Spring Plantation, Stanton Hall symbolizes the latter stage of that run. Frederick Stanton poured most of his cotton-generated fortune into the house he would call Belfast. Like a massive wedding cake perched on an entire city block of downtown Natchez, Stanton Hall is so richly detailed and so overwhelming in scale that it can't be fully appreciated on a single visit. And it's not even the largest or, by some standards, the finest of Mississippi's antebellum homes. For six decades, when money flowed through Natchez,

Woodville, Columbus, and Holly Springs like mud off a cotton furrow after a hard spring rain, it seemed that the manors and mansions of the nabobs and the newly rich simply couldn't be built any larger or any grander. But somehow they were. The simplicity of Cold Spring and Rosemont and the Feltus-Catchings House gave way to the opulence of Riverview and Athenia and Melrose. Those were houses to rival any in America of the 1840s and 1850s, but the one-upmanship wasn't over yet. As civil war and ruin crept closer and closer, men like Frederick Stanton of Belfast, Charles Dahlgren of Dunleith, Haller Nutt of Longwood, and Smith Daniell of Windsor turned blind eyes to the gathering storm and ordered ever more European furniture, more carved plaster, deeper moldings, and higher ceilings, in a final frantic burst of devil-may-care opulence.

Between the simplicity of Cold Spring and the overwhelming grandeur of Stanton Hall, hundreds of mansions and near-mansions were built throughout Mississippi. Many are now gone; those that remain are

an architectural timeline, tracing the development of what was once the farthest, most sparsely settled corner of the new nation into a rich and influential state. The oldest houses, of course, are concentrated in a narrow band running up the Mississippi River from Woodville to Port Gibson. As pioneers ventured farther inland from the river and Indian lands were sold off, the towns and the plantations and the inevitable wealth followed. Natchez would always be the pacesetter in architectural matters, but it was eventually rivaled by Holly Springs, Aberdeen, Columbus, and Vicksburg, among others.

It all started soon after Mississippi was folded into the fledgling United States of America. In 1798, when Spain deeded the Mississippi Territory over to the United States government, this land from which Mississippi and Alabama would be carved was essentially empty. The Choctaw and Chickasaw Indians would cling to their tribal lands for another two to three decades. Except for settlements along the lower Mississippi River and the Gulf Coast, the territory was a vast blank space, waiting to be filled with adventurous farmers and entrepreneurs. The few existing homes were mainly log cabins and dogtrots, with a scattering of nicer homes in Natchez and Woodville, styled on a West Indian model with masonry main levels, frame upper stories, and exterior stairs.

Over the ensuing decades, all the elements that would transform first Natchez, and, later, Mississippi as a whole, into an antebellum architectural wonderland meshed. Surrounded by rich cotton lands and perched on flood-proof bluffs, Natchez grew from the shanties under the hill, fueled by Eli Whitney's cotton gins and Robert Fulton's steamboats lined up at the wharves. Planters and bankers and cotton brokers found themselves with riches beyond their wildest dreams, and they early on established a legacy of plowing those riches back into bricks and mortar. The old West Indian–styled houses such as Concord and the House on Ellicott's Hill gave way to the more popular Federal fashion, first at Auburn and Gloucester, with their strict symmetry and massive columns. Within a few years, they were joined by Rosalie, Arlington, Linden, Mount Repose, and numerous others. Downriver, in Woodville and Pinckneyville, and upriver, in Church Hill, Rodney, and Port Gibson, Federal-style houses were also dominant.

By the 1830s, Federal architecture was losing its appeal, and was being gradually replaced by Greek Revival. In the South as a whole and Mississippi in particular, Greek Revival would dominate domestic building choices for the next thirty years. Thus, the decades that gave American architecture some of its most memorable houses were the very ones when Mississippi was riding an economic crest that rarely sagged. Newcomers poured into the northern and eastern sections of the state, scooping up cheap Indian lands offered for sale by the federal government. Natchez still set the pace, both culturally and financially, but it was increasingly rivaled by new towns like Holly Springs, Aberdeen, Columbus, Enterprise, and Canton. If the nabobs in Natchez could boast of Homewood, Magnolia Hill, and D'evereux, Holly Springs could match them brick for brick with Montrose, Strawberry Plains, and Athenia. Columbus and Aberdeen rode the Tombigbee River's prosperity in the northeastern part of the state, demonstrating their culture with Riverview, the Magnolias, Waverley, and Camellia Place. With its river-based economy, Vicksburg had surpassed even Natchez and Jackson, and it showed in the construction of Balfour House, Cedar Grove, Anchuca, and the Duff Green House. Port Gibson claimed the grandest palace of them all, the inimitable but short-lived Windsor.

Building trends waxed and waned with the economic times, slowing when cotton prices drooped or a financial panic set in, but never really stopping during the years between 1830 and 1860. The Italianate and Gothic styles made slight inroads into Mississippi, most notably with Annandale and Ingleside in Madison County, Rosedale in Columbus, the Manship House in Jackson, and the landmark Gothic houses of Holly Springs, Cedarhurst and Airliewood. As the building bubble neared the bursting point in the 1850s, architects blended Greek Revival, Italianate, and Gothic details at will, almost as if they couldn't completely decide on which style to emphasize. Italianate brackets were slipped beneath the eaves over Greek Revival columns, and sharp Gothic arches added a unique touch to the verandas of otherwise classical homes. Spires Boling, the premier architect of antebellum Holly Springs, delighted in the insertion of octagonal forms throughout his houses, most notably in the unique towers of Walter Place. Columbus architects gracefully merged a conglomerate of stylistic elements into the Columbus Eclectic movement.

In the last few years before the Civil War, mansion building reached a remarkably frenzied pace, a harbinger that this precarious society built on slave labor and eroding topsoil was realizing that its days were numbered. Houses grew to almost baronial size, with twenty or more rooms, sixteen-foot ceilings, and lawns stretching away for acres. Windsor, Dunleith, and Stanton Hall were scaled beyond anything imaginable to the average American. Interior and exterior details were piled on like icing, and spacious parlors and bedrooms were packed wall to wall with imported furniture. Cotton prices were high, labor was cheap, and southern congressmen were blustering about states' rights, secession, and the permanence of slavery, that "peculiar institution." All over Mississippi, the sound of hammers and the smoke from brick kilns were ever present. But the bubble was about to burst.

Longwood, more than any other house in Mississippi, symbolizes the abrupt termination of the architectural boom in the state. Its empty, echoing floors and dusty carpenter's tools are mute witnesses to the flight of the northern workmen who abandoned their jobs at the onset of the Civil War. Dr. Haller Nutt had eagerly sought out Philadelphia architect Samuel Sloan and convinced him that he had the resources and the determination to see Sloan's outrageous "Oriental Villa" brought to reality. The project began with high hopes and the certainty on Dr. Nutt's part that his home would outshine and outlast all others in Natchez or anywhere else in Mississippi. Within months of ground breaking, though, Mississippi was out of the Union. Sloan's workers fled for their lives, leaving behind a genteel thank-you note with the local newspaper. Longwood would never be finished, and Mississippi would never again lead the nation in architectural innovation. An entire generation of young men left for Antietam and Gettysburg and Shiloh and were not seen again. Longwood stayed dark. Decades of architectural changes, encompassing the late Italianate, Victorian Gothic, and Second Empire styles, were barely evident in Mississippi.

It would be seventy years after Haller Nutt's dream collapsed before Mississippians realized that they still possessed a legacy that the rest of the country would pay to see. Dozens of the old mansions had burned, fallen in, or been chopped into sharecropper quarters in the last years of the nineteenth century and early years of the twentieth. The old cotton money was gone, but boards still needed painting, roofs had to be replaced, and sixteen-foot-high ceilings made more than one dusty parlor too hard to heat. In some cases, the dwindling family members just walked away from these white elephants that they couldn't afford to maintain any longer. George Hampton Young's masterpiece, Waverley, was left a fully furnished relic by his last surviving son in 1913. It slowly vanished into the woods of Clay County, doors wide open and no inhabitants but dirt daubers, bats, and raccoons for fifty years. Other mansions were perilously close to oblivion when the ladies of Natchez reluctantly opened their doors for Depression-era tours. The "pilgrimage" tradition was born, and more than one of the great houses was saved by vast infusions of tourist dollars. Even Longwood was salvaged and now draws thousands of fascinated visitors in any given year.

Many of those visitors come to admire the architectural beauty and perfection of Natchez and Vicksburg, Columbus and Holly Springs. They may not realize that what they are witnessing is a truly unique reflection of a society and a culture that flourished for a few brief decades but left Mississippi with treasures that can never be replaced.

Federal Style

America was a very young nation when the Mississippi Territory was added to it in 1798. It was a democracy struggling to establish its legitimacy and hammer out the details of honoring the ideals presented in the Constitution, with little time or energy left over for such ethereal pursuits as architecture and design. In the fifteen years that had passed since the end of the Revolution, the nation had produced no distinct building styles that could truly be considered "American." The public buildings of the planned capital city, Washington, D.C., were laid out by a Frenchman, Pierre L'Enfant. Domestic architecture, where it evolved beyond the simplest log dogtrot or cabin, was a reflection of the Old World houses such as Cape Cod saltboxes, Dutch colonials, and a few Georgian mansions along the Atlantic Coast.

British tastes were turning to the work of the Adam brothers of Scotland. Their styles had emerged as a more refined, lighter, and highly symmetrical version of the Georgian fashion that had dominated eighteenth-century Britain. Georgian architecture had

been an outgrowth of the designs of Andrea Palladio, a Renaissance Italian architect who delved deep into ancient history for his architectural forms. He rejuvenated the classical forms of columns, pediments, entablatures, and geometric symmetry. The Adam style took those classical elements and melded them into a tradition that would influence the entire Western world for half a century.

As the lands that would someday be Mississippi and Alabama entered the Union, the time was ripe for American architecture to bloom. Inspired by pattern books, frontier carpenters and a few trained architects borrowed the forms and details of Adam styling and began to fill the nation's cities and countryside with its first fine mansions and town houses. Relations with

the British were strained, and no one wanted to credit the English or the Scots with flattery by imitation. So the Adam style was Americanized and dubbed "Federal," and it would be the choice of those with money to spare. As the nation grew, new courthouses and statehouses and banks and churches were built with Federal lines. Gradually, domestic architecture followed, with the mansions of New England, Virginia, and the Carolinas imitating the pattern.

During the dominant period of Federal styling, the years from 1780 to 1830, the only significant settlements in Mississippi were along the Mississippi River and the Gulf Coast. Natchez was little more than a motley collection of log houses and dogtrots in 1790; ten years later, as the cultural, political, and economic capital of the Mississippi Territory, it was evolving into a true town. The appearance of Eli Whitney's cotton gin (1794) and the arrival of the first steamboats at Natchez Under-the-Hill (1811) heralded the dawn of the Cotton Kingdom, a sixty-year era when Natchez would come to boast more wealth than almost any other city in America. As planters and local business-men began to accumulate unheard-of riches, the need for fine houses and public buildings became evident. The Federal style fit the bill perfectly, with its ostentatious columns and solidity, and it was that style that first came to symbolize the allure of Natchez.

There had been a few grand houses in Natchez even before the Federal era. Most were built on a French/West Indian model, with a masonry ground level, often devoted to storage and support areas. Above would be a frame second story with living quarters. The rooms frequently opened directly onto a gallery with no central hall or interior stair, as at Concord and the House on Ellicott's Hill. Town houses of the late 1700s and very early 1800s, such as Texada, were brick structures with some detailing, situated very close to the road. But as cotton money rolled into Natchez and the community recognized its need for public structures and private homes, those with the means to build anything they desired turned to the Federal style. The same would hold true in other river communities, such as Woodville, Pinckneyville, Church Hill, and Port Gibson.

Those with the skill to create Federal details and follow a pattern book were the men of the hour. Levi Weeks was a Massachusetts native whose 1809 trial for murder ended in acquittal but left his reputation in tatters. He transplanted his talents at carpentry and design across the country to Natchez, advertising

his services as a maker of chairs and cabinets. Banker/lawyer Lyman Harding, also a Massachusetts expatriate, hired him to construct what Weeks would call "the first house in the Territory on which was ever attempted any of the orders of Architecture."[1] Ground was broken for Auburn in 1812; in its finished form, it would represent most dramatically the Federal style in Mississippi and influence southern architecture for decades to come. The house incorporates all of the classical elements of Federal architecture. A full-height four-columned portico supports a triangular pediment with a central oval lunette. The columns are Roman Doric, topped with Ionic capitals. Behind the portico, the doorways are centered in an elaborately carved frontispiece with curving fanlights and rectangular sidelights. Windows are rigidly arranged symmetrically, both vertically and horizontally. The cornice line features carved dentils. Later additions increased the facade to seven bays from the original five.

Weeks utilized popular pattern books, copying the portico from Abraham Swan's 1757 *Collection of Designs in Architecture* and the interior geometric stair, the fanlights, and the capitals from William Pain's *British Palladio,* also published in 1757. He would go on to build the East Wing of Jefferson College, the original Presbyterian Church of Natchez, Natchez Hospital, and the Bank of Mississippi, all Federal-style structures, before dying of yellow fever in 1819.

Lewis House (above) and Rosalie typify Federal architecture

The race was on, a crescendo of architectural competition that wouldn't peak for almost fifty years. Other Natchez builders noticed Weeks's ideas and artistry at Auburn and produced increasingly grand Federal mansions for the next two decades. The Forest, the Briars, Linden, Arlington, and Clifton went up. On the bluff close by the site of the old French fort, Rosalie demonstrated a refinement of Auburn's style. As at Auburn, Rosalie is dominated by the full-height portico, fronted by four Tuscan columns with a delicate connecting balustrade. The three central bays are stuccoed and flanked by red brick bays on each side. The elliptical fanlights crown the upper and lower front doors and an oval window is centered in the pediment.

Public buildings in the early years of Natchez followed the Federal form as well. The 1827 Masonic Hall was a massive downtown structure with engaged Corinthian columns and pilasters, a central projecting pavilion rather than a full portico. Churches were Federal inspired, as were banks, courthouses, and hospitals.

In the era of Federal-style dominance, which lasted until approximately 1830, only the towns of southwest Mississippi were advanced enough economically to feature these houses. Woodville has several surviving examples, including the rare frame Feltus-Catchings House and the Lewis House. Several of the oldest Port Gibson houses show a Federal influence as well. Biloxi, Pass Christian, and Columbus developed in the very last days of Federal popularity, and a few of their houses incorporated details such as elliptical fanlights and windowed pediments, even as the shift to Greek Revival began. Indian cession towns such as Oxford, Aberdeen, Canton, and Macon missed the Federal period altogether, although an occasional house of the 1830s and 1840s will include a Federal detail in its predominately Greek Revival theme.

By the late 1820s, American disillusionment with all things British and the country's fascination with Greek and Roman archeological discoveries shifted the creative emphasis to a style that was even more classically inspired than the Federal. The resulting Greek Revival trend would borrow significant features from the Federal era, including the dominating columns and porticoes. As it evolved over the thirty years immediately before the Civil War, Greek Revival would come to symbolize southern architecture as no other style has before or since. The old Federal homes would be modified and modernized, but most that survived over the next century retained the elements that mark them as the very earliest examples of Mississippi's antebellum artistic endeavors.

COLD SPRING

Woodville is a hidden jewel deep in southwest Mississippi. Other than its neighbor to the east, Centreville, it is the only real town remaining in Wilkinson County. This historic corner of the state was home to some of the Mississippi Territory's first settlers, who founded Fort Adams, Pinckneyville, and Pond. Those communities have long since dried up, leaving only road signs and the ancient store at Pond, but the old homes that sheltered their long-dead founders still dot the countryside near the Louisiana border and the Mississippi River. Some, like the Wall House and Salisbury, are sinking into oblivion, slowly receding into the deep gulleys and creeping vegetation that grows unchecked over the years. Others, like Cold Spring, stand almost unchanged over two centuries, still home to descendants of those first pioneers who chose this far outpost of the territory as their own.

Cold Spring was built by Dr. John Carmichael, a surgeon in the army of General James Wilkinson. Wilkinson was a shadowy figure who may have conspired with Aaron Burr in his treasonous intrigues of the early nineteenth century. He gave his name to the county formed in 1802 and left his surgeon with land near Pinckneyville. Dr. Carmichael may have begun building Cold Spring by 1804. The lines of the house date it as one of the oldest in the state, as evidenced by the unusual, West Indian–style roof and front gable with an intricately carved semicircular lunette. The two lower levels are fronted by full-width galleries, later screened upstairs. Iron railings connect four Tuscan columns. The overall style is Federal, typical of the period, but the main entrance has rectangular transoms and sidelights, more suggestive of the Greek Revival phase which appeared twenty years after Cold Spring was built. On the rear, a two-story archway has been enclosed by the addition of more modern rooms.

The interior of Cold Spring is simple, indicative of a country home built for security and function rather than ostentatious display. The central hallway is undecorated and opens to two formal rooms. The stair is simple and rises from a rear alcove, serving strictly as a means of reaching the second floor rather than as a decoration. Upstairs are bedrooms and added baths. On the rear of the house, in the space created by the enclosed archway, are a den and kitchen. The original railing which once kept animals out of the arched entranceway is now a fence.

Cold Spring's setting is one of the most memorable in Mississippi. A long sunken road leads through woods and ancient rosebushes, opening finally into a pasture. The house is almost hidden by massive live oaks, ten-foot-tall azaleas, and curtains of Spanish moss. The trees seem to have encircled the house, protecting it from sight and lending an air of mystery.

The atmosphere around Cold Spring is indeed one of mystery, supplying two of the most infamous "ghosts" in Mississippi architectural lore. Legend tells of Dr. Carmichael's wine cellar, his pride and joy, where he would rock in his favorite chair and drink with friends for hours on end. When he died, he had left instructions for those friends to consume the rest of his horde before they buried him. They followed his wishes, stumbled off with the coffin, and prompt-

Cold Spring's cantilevered roofline marks it as one of Mississippi's oldest houses.

ly forgot where they had buried the doctor. When sober, they managed to locate the grave, and Dr. Carmichael was reinterred with a bit more dignity in Woodville. For years, it was told that the sound of a rocking chair squeaking came from the old wine cellar. The cellar caved in years ago; when the current owners were having termite treatments done in the remains of the basement, workers turned up a thick, beveled plank of wood, bearing the elaborately scripted words "Doct. John Carmichael, Care of," most likely the lid of a whiskey keg delivered two hundred years ago. The eerie squeaking sounds have not been heard lately.

Dr. Carmichael's nephew inherited Cold Spring after the surgeon's death. In 1840, the house was sold to Judge Edward McGehee of Woodville, owner of Bowling Green and the renowned McGehee Mills. Judge McGehee gave the property to his son, Edward, and Cold Spring has since been enjoyed by six generations of descendants. Somewhere in that lineage, a jilted young lady pined away and became the legendary "face in the window." Servants first noticed the image of the dead girl on the glass of her bedroom window; over the years, the story took on a life of its own and attracted scores of curious gawkers. Worn out with the intrusion on her privacy, the mistress of

the house smashed the window and put an end to that ghostly tale.

The current owners, Mary Katherine and Jimmie Randall, don't put much stock in the strange tales connected with Cold Spring. They faithfully tend to the cracks in the plaster and the constant yard work required by the vast grounds, welcoming guests who venture twenty miles and two centuries off the main road to enjoy the hospitality of one of Mississippi's most unique homes.

Cold Spring is surrounded by moss-draped live oaks.

AUBURN

Natchez was just on the cusp of its meteoric rise to wealth when Auburn was built. The first steamboats were lining up several deep at the wharves jutting out from Natchez Under-the-Hill, disgorging enterprising newcomers and loading up the cotton that would flood southwest Mississippi with a half-century of previously unimagined prosperity. The mansions above the bluffs are the enduring symbols of that era, and none is more architecturally significant or historically rich than Auburn. In a fascinating twist of history, its story is largely that of one man who labored to peacefully dismantle the very slave system that built this house and most of its neighbors.

In 1812, architect Levi Weeks was three years beyond flight from his native Massachusetts, where his reputation and career had nose-dived after he was charged with murdering his fiancée. Even after his acquittal, the charge followed him like a curse, and he boarded a steamboat bound for Natchez, hoping to reestablish himself in this booming corner of America, far from New England and his accusers. He brought

his designing and carpentry skills to Mississippi and opened a cabinetry and chair shop. It was a fortunate decision for the young builder, for his skills would make an impact on American architecture that would still be evident two hundred years later.

Lyman Harding was also a native of Massachusetts, one who had arrived in Natchez under happier circumstances. His position as director of the powerful Bank of Mississippi and his law practice led to financial success, and in 1812 he contracted with Levi Weeks to build a new house for his family. Weeks combined his natural talents with patterns pulled from popular design books, creating a house that eclipsed any standing in Natchez. Most homes in existence in 1812 were similar to Concord, heavily influenced by French and West Indian building styles, and typically having a masonry base level with a raised frame living area. The house that Weeks would build for Lyman Harding was drastically and dramatically different. He wrote of it to his friend, Ep Hoyt, back home in Massachusetts:

Levi Weeks's "geometrical staircase" is a masterpiece of design and skillful carpentry.

The brick house I am building is just without the city limits and is designed for the most magnificent building in the Territory. The body of this house is 60 by 45 feet with a portico of 31 feet projecting 12 feet supported by 4 Ionic columns with the Corinthian entablature, the ceiling vaulted, the house two stories with a geometrical staircase to ascend to the second story. This is the first house in the Territory on which was ever attempted any of the orders of Architecture. The site is one of those peculiar situations which combines all the delight of romance, the pleasure of rurality, and the approach of sublimity. I am the more particular in describing this seat not only to give you an idea of the progress of improvement but to inform you what you will hear with pleasure, that the owner of it is a Yankey [sic], a native of our own state, Massachusetts, and is now in Boston on a visit. His name is Lyman Harding.[2]

When completed, Auburn was unique in its grandeur and perfection. Its two-story portico with massive columns predated even the porticoes of the University of Virginia and the White House, influencing the style of untold numbers of Federal and Greek Revival mansions which would follow, not only in Natchez but throughout Mississippi and the South. Weeks borrowed freely from pattern books, modeling the front entrance on Abraham Swan's *Collection of Designs in Architecture* and taking the column capitals

Left: The entrance to Auburn is copied from an Abraham Swan design.
Right: The original five-bay facade of Auburn was expanded with two wings in 1827.

from William Pain's *British Palladio*, both published in the eighteenth century. The interior was as elegant as the exterior, with a "geometrical staircase" and swan's neck pediments crowning the interior doorways.

Lyman Harding died within a few years of Auburn's completion. His widow rented the house to a young doctor, Stephen Duncan, who had moved to Natchez after completing medical school in Pennsylvania in 1808. Duncan was related to several of the most influential families in Natchez, and he had increased his community standing by marrying Margaret Ellis in 1816. Her dowry included rich bottomlands along the Homochitto River, which Duncan turned into cotton plantations. After her death, he married yet another rich Natchez heiress, Catherine Bingaman. In addition to his cotton empire, he succeeded his uncle, Samuel Postlethwaite, as president of the Bank of Mississippi. With all these financial windfalls, he bought Auburn outright from Harding's estate in 1820. Seven years later, he added the symmetrical wings to the main house block and also added on to the rear, as well as building a Greek Revival billiard hall adjacent to the main house.

Duncan accumulated land and slaves at an extraordinary clip. At the peak of his empire, he was reputed to be the world's largest slave owner and cotton producer: six cotton plantations, two sugar plantations, and more than one thousand slaves were under his direction. Annually, his land produced over four thousand bales of cotton and three thousand hogsheads of sugar. Auburn alone required twenty-three servants to keep it running. Dr. Duncan also owned land in Issaquena, Jefferson, and Adams counties in Mississippi as well as extensive acreage in Louisiana. By 1856, his wealth was estimated at a phenomenal $1.9 million.

Duncan was conflicted by slavery and even more so by the unresolved problems of "free men of color," viewed by even the most enlightened southerners as threats to their dominance. Along with several other Natchez leaders, he formed the Mississippi Colonization Society in 1831. It was an arm of the American Colonization Society, and its purpose was to send freed slaves to Liberia, where they would be supported by funds from the society until they were able to provide for their own needs. Duncan became embroiled in the twelve-year court battle over settlement of the will of his friend, Isaac Ross. Ross wished to have his slaves manumitted and sent back to Africa, but his heirs at Prospect Hill Plantation fought tooth and nail to block the will's implementation. Duncan took great personal risk in smuggling seventy-two of those slaves onto a midnight steamboat:

In March, 1844, the brig Lime Rock *sailed from the Crescent City with another large contingent of the Ross slaves. Ninety-two Mississippi free Negroes accompanied this voyage; all but twenty of these were from the Ross estate. The opposition in Natchez against the further transportation of the Ross slaves was so intense that Dr. Duncan was obliged to hide the potential emigrants on an isolated section of the Mississippi River while they awaited steamboat passage to New Orleans. Upon arriving in Liberia, most of these Ross slaves settled with their comrades in the community of Reedsville, some five miles up the Sinou River from Greenville.*[3]

Eventually, between two hundred and fifty and three hundred of Ross's slaves made their way to Liberia, largely through the persistence of Stephen Duncan.

Duncan vigorously and vocally opposed secession. Auburn was not damaged during the Civil War, but Duncan left in despair in 1863, dying four years later in his native New England. His son, also named Stephen, lived sporadically at Auburn, often leaving it in the hands of servants. A turn-of-the-century visitor recalled being greeted at the door by one of these servants and noticing that the parlor wallpaper was peeling away. In 1910, the younger Stephen Duncan died, having willed the house to his nephews. They deeded the property to the city of Natchez in 1911. Duncan Park was created around the mansion, which is meticulously overseen by the Auburn Garden Club.

ROSEMONT

Jefferson Davis was chosen as the first and only president of the Confederate States of America by the Confederate Congress in February 1861. A telegram flashed from Montgomery to Vicksburg, where a rider was dispatched across the narrow neck of land connecting Davis Bend to Warren County. He found the recently resigned senator tending the roses that trailed along the fences around Brierfield, the Davis plantation. Davis read the telegram to his wife, who would recall that Davis's expression was that of "a man [who] might speak of a sentence of death."[4]

Davis would not see his rosebushes again for many years, and he never again lived for any length of time at Brierfield. He may have planted the roses originally as a reminder of his boyhood home, an inauspicious but comfortable house deep in a grove of poplar trees, just outside Woodville. That house would come to be known as Rosemont in honor of the bushes Davis's mother planted and tended, and which brought color and aroma to the landscape.

Davis's father, Samuel Emory Davis, was a nomadic sort. He moved his family, which eventually included ten children, from Georgia to South Carolina, Kentucky (where Jefferson was the last born, trailing his brother Joseph by twenty-five years), and then to Bayou Teche, Louisiana, in 1810. The malarial swamps there quickly ran him north to Mississippi, where he selected a beautiful site just east of Woodville. At the end of his life, Jefferson Davis recalled the place that would, for him, symbolize his childhood: "[My father] found a place that suited him about one mile east of Woodville, in Wilkinson County, Mississippi. He removed his family there, and it is there that my memories begin."[5]

It is an irony of history that the man who would come to symbolize the South's struggle to maintain its slaveholding caste system was not born to an aristocratic family. Samuel Davis was never a wealthy man. He probably leased the Wilkinson County land initially, working it with his few slaves (never more than a dozen) and his sons. When he was settled enough to build a house, it was typical of the late-Federal architecture of the day but on a much more modest scale than the homes appearing thirty miles north in Natchez. Originally called Poplar Grove, the house is a one-and-a-half-story frame structure raised on three-foot-tall brick piers. An undercut gallery stretches the entire length of the five-bay front facade, topped by a central gable with a Palladian window. Two dormers flank the central gable. Along the gallery, square wooden balustrades connect the simple box columns. The

Rosemont's portico incorporates a Palladian window.

front entrance is a large double door framed by rectangular sidelights and transom. The entire exterior is sheathed in cypress clapboards, painted brown. Another gallery is found on the back, with two interior chimneys which originally connected to all six fireplaces. Before the house was even finished, Jane Davis had begun planting the dozens of rosebushes which would eventually give the place its name.

Inside, a wide central hallway separates two rooms on each side of the main floor. Ornamentation is lacking, with only a floral ceiling medallion in the hall. Upstairs, two rooms and a sitting room are tucked under the gabled roof.

All in all, it is a handsome but functional farmhouse, rather than a mansion. Jefferson Davis grew up there, walking into Woodville daily to attend a small log cabin school. Concerned that his youngest son was not being adequately educated, Samuel sent him off to Kentucky's St. Thomas College in 1816, when the boy was barely eight years old. Yielding to Jane's protests, Samuel brought him home two years later. Jefferson College was functioning in nearby Washington, Mississippi, and Samuel and Jane compromised on that choice. When Wilkinson County Academy opened soon after, Jefferson could finally live at home again. He would then remain at Rosemont until leaving for Transylvania University in 1823. From that point on, he would never again live at Rosemont for any extended period of time.

By the time Jefferson headed off to Kentucky, his father had lost title to Rosemont. A loan he backed for a son-in-law went unpaid, and Joseph Davis had to buy the property to keep it from being lost to the family altogether. Joseph never fully paid his part, however, and the house and land wound up in the hands of his sister Lucinda and her husband, William Stamps. William was a successful landowner, bank director, and states' rights advocate, and he managed to hang on to Rosemont. The elder Davises lived on there while Jefferson was a student at West Point; Samuel died in 1824.

As his military and political career gained prominence, Jefferson Davis's visits to Rosemont became more and more infrequent. His first wife, daughter of President Zachary Taylor, never even visited the homeplace in the three brief months that she and Jefferson were married before her death. He brought his second bride, Varina Howell, to Rosemont soon after their 1845 marriage in Natchez, seeing his mother for the last time. The Stamps family lived on in the house, their descendants caring for it until 1896. It went through several changes of ownership during the twentieth century. For thirty years, it has been preserved and restored by Percival Beacroft, Jr., and Ernesto Caldeira. The descendants of Jefferson and Varina Davis hold frequent reunions, returning to enjoy Jane's roses and the peaceful isolation of Rosemont.

Samuel Davis's Rosemont was the first home Jefferson Davis remembered.

ROSALIE

—Natchez

In 1716, French explorer Jean-Baptiste Le Moyne, Sieur de Bienville, chose a site high on the bluffs overlooking the Mississippi River to build Fort Rosalie, naming the tiny fortification in honor of the Countess of Ponchartrain. The crude fort stood for thirteen years as relations between the French settlers and the Natchez Indians deteriorated, culminating in a bloody massacre of the Europeans in 1729. The site was abandoned until the British acquired it in 1783, renaming it Fort Panmure. It was little used and given over to the Spaniards in 1779. When the Spanish left Natchez for good in 1798, the ruins became the property of the American government. A patent for almost twenty-two acres, encompassing the ruins of the old fort, was soon after granted to Henry Willis. More than two decades would pass before a house would be built on the site.

Natchez was barely a town by any standard in 1798. A few decent houses rode the bluff, and Natchez Under-the-Hill was more than a decade away from its heyday, when dozens of steamboats would dock there to unload cargo, pile on bales of cotton, and disgorge passengers and crew eager for the seamier side of life. As the rough-and-tumble village gradually developed into a real town, fueled by cotton's profits, its first building boom emerged. One of the many northern transplants to Natchez, Peter Little, was prescient enough to see that boom developing; his sawmill would be the first in Natchez. Apocryphal stories tell of Little lurking about the waterfront, dragging abandoned wood from sunken boats back to his mill. In whatever manner he got his start, within a few years he was one of the most successful businessmen in Natchez. He was a prosperous bachelor when he found himself the guardian of young Eliza Low, orphaned in a yellow fever epidemic. Not knowing what else to do, Little married Eliza, who may have been as young as thirteen, and sent her packing to a finishing school up north.

Eliza Low Little returned several years later as a "finished" young woman, inspiring Peter Little to purchase the old Fort Rosalie tract and begin plans for a mansion. He sold the south half of the lot, including the fort site, reserving the northern edge on the bluffs for his house's location. Construction began around 1820. Little hired his brother-in-law, James S. Griffin of Baltimore, to superintend the project as architect. Modeled on the lines of Levi Weeks's 1812 Auburn, Rosalie was designed as a Federal-style mansion, two-and-one-half stories above a full basement, red brick in a near-perfect cube. The five-bay front facade is fronted by a full-height portico and four tapered Tuscan columns, crowned by a pediment with a sunburst-design oval window. Fanlighted doorways open on upper and lower galleries, front and rear. Reflecting Little's ability to obtain the finest and most durable woods, the floors of the front porch and balcony are painted cypress; the rear gallery is floored with painted canvas on top of cypress. The four steps leading from the rear terrace to the gallery are whole cypress logs.

Inside, the artistry of antebellum craftsmen in early Natchez is evident. A central hallway divides the dou-

Peter Little built Rosalie on the bluffs overlooking the Mississippi River.

ble parlors on the east side from the library, stair hall, and dining room on the west. Fourteen-inch-thick walls are plastered and painted; heart cypress floors are stained to a dark sheen. The mahogany stair loops continuously from the first floor to the third-story attic. That attic also has cypress flooring, plastered walls, and light streaming in from the pediment window, a skylight, and a rear dormer.

Another notable feature of Rosalie is the cypress picket fence, held together by expert joinery, with no nails or pegs. It withstood the winds of an 1840 tornado which destroyed much of Natchez. That storm splintered the original square cupola atop Rosalie, which Peter Little replaced with an observation deck.

Peter and Eliza Little moved into Rosalie in 1823. An observer that year described the recently completed house: "On the right to the south, it is a noble colonnaded structure whose heavy appearance is gracefully relieved by shrubbery, parterres of roses, and a light latticed summerhouse. The summerhouse crowns an eminence in the rear, and is half suspended over a three hundred foot precipice overlooking the Mississippi River. Between this and the forest background, rise the romantic ruins of Fort Rosalie."[6]

The Littles remained childless, and Eliza spent much of her time tending to the itinerant Methodist preachers who frequently stopped in Natchez. When Peter tired of constantly finding ministers at his table, he built the Parsonage across the street and shuttled Eliza's visitors out the door. Eliza died in 1853, followed three years later by Peter, and the estate sold the house to Andrew Wilson and his wife. The Wilsons commissioned extensive interior renovations, adding marble mantels and elaborate plaster medallions.

When Union gunboats docked below the Natchez bluffs, the town quickly capitulated and absorbed the Union officers into their social set. Andrew Wilson had scurried to Texas with his slaves, hoping to wait out the conflict and retain his workforce. Mrs. Wilson and her adopted daughter, Fannie McMurtry, were left to tend Rosalie. The elegance of the house, along with its strategic position overlooking the river, made it the logical choice for quartering Union commanders. General and Mrs. Ulysses Grant moved in first, followed by General and Mrs. Walter Q. Gresham. Gresham was an Indianan, and his wife was from a secessionist family in Kentucky, so they had little trouble making friends throughout Natchez, especially the Wilsons. Natchez neighbors dropped by the Wilsons' to visit with these intriguing new arrivals. Mrs. Gresham recalled that "Much cheer, many cigars and toddies [were] at these headquarters . . . Hospitable by nature, these men were almost universally cordial to my husband."[7] She even learned to play poker.

Not all went smoothly during Federal occupation. Having heard stories from around the state about pillage and destruction, Mrs. Wilson had ordered Rosalie's enormous pier mirrors boxed up and buried on the lawn, along with the sterling silver and other valuables. As time went on, rumors spread among the Union officers that she might be a Confederate spy, and she was briefly arrested and jailed on suspicion of espionage. She was eventually released, most of the the valuables were dug up and returned to the house, and the Wilsons and Greshams maintained a long and enduring friendship.

Rosalie survived the war unscathed and passed through several generations of the Wilson family. Like most of the mansions of Natchez, it had fallen on hard times by the 1930s. In 1938, the local chapter of the Daughters of the American Revolution took on the house as a restoration and preservation project, and it has been meticulously overseen by that organization. Even after sixty years of care, Rosalie still yields secrets and treasures. In 2003, Peter Little's checkbooks were discovered in an attic wall, adding to the historic value of one the most enduring sites in Natchez.

FELTUS-CATCHINGS HOUSE

—Woodville

Looming over the southwest corner of South and Depot streets in downtown Woodville, the Feltus-Catchings House seems almost too massive to squeeze onto the lot. It has stood on this site since the mid-1820s, witnessing the growth of Woodville from a tiny, isolated outpost in the years of early statehood, through its boom years before and after the Civil War, to the quiet place it occupies today in the far southwestern corner of the state. The house is a rare and graceful example of Federal styling, unique for the region in its frame construction and noted for the detail work of its facade.

Mississippi was less than two years past its territorial days when Abram Scott bought this lot from Asa Sapp. Scott most likely built the house and lived there for just a few years, dividing his time among Woodville, the old capital city at Washington, and the new center of government, Jackson. He helped to write the original 1817 constitution, served two terms as lieutenant governor, and was elected governor in 1831. Under his direction, the legislature wrote a new 1832 constitution, which he saw adopted before his death in 1833.

Scott had sold the Woodville house before his rise in political circles. Prestwood Smith purchased what must have been the finest house in town during the 1820s, a two-and-a-half-story mansion with monumental Tuscan columns supporting a central pediment. Centered in the middle of five bays is an elaborate doorway with a broad elliptical fanlight and rectangular sidelights. A balcony with wooden balustrade is suspended above the entrance; originally, it stretched the length of the facade.

Smith was a tavernkeeper who lived to enjoy his fine house for only three years after its purchase. He was murdered in his tavern in 1829, and the house passed through a series of owners before it was sold at a courthouse auction to Abram M. Feltus twelve years later. Feltus was a New York native who had built a successful career as a businessman and banker during his thirty years in Woodville. He died at the onset of the Civil War and his house began a slow decline. By 1886, it had been converted to a boardinghouse, run by a Mrs. Smith. She advertised widely in the Woodville newspapers:

Are you hungry? Are you weary? Go right to Mrs. G. F. Smith at the Feltus House, where you can find a first-class table, supplied with the very best the market affords: neat and comfortable beds, pleasant rooms, and attentive servants . . . We make a specialty of having a strictly first-class vegetable garden, affording all standard varieties in abundance.[8]

In 1900, the boardinghouse was purchased by Dr. Charles Catchings, who had opened a medical practice in Woodville in 1894. For the next eighty-five years, there would be a Dr. Catchings at home on this corner, evidenced by the name carved into a square of cement fronting the house. The Catchings family converted the mansion back into a private home, which has remained with them for several generations. It still dominates its corner lot; behind it are quiet gardens and a one-story dependency.

LEWIS HOUSE

—Woodville

In the 1930s, WPA photographers fanned out across Mississippi and the South, training their Roloflexes and Yashicas on the crumbling mansions of the ante-bellum era. This make-work project for starving artists not only served the immediate purpose of providing jobs but also generated the most complete and, in some cases, the only record of Mississippi's great mansions. Many were lost over the next few decades, their imminent demise chillingly apparent in those stark black-and-white photographs.

To look at the WPA photo of Woodville's Lewis House would be to assume that it was in its last days, like so many of its contemporaries. In that photo, the century-old mansion is in decrepit shape. The portico is devoid of paint, although the narrow elliptical fanlight retains its delicate carving. Shutters are drooping and slats are missing altogether in some. The front door stands open beneath the Federal-style fanlight, with some sort of furniture seen in the main hallway. The yard is overgrown and neglected, and the entire picture is one of decaying grandeur.

Thankfully, appearances are not always predictive of the future. When the photo was taken, the Lewis House had already been standing for more than one hundred years. It was built by Dr. Thomas Lynne on acreage originally owned by Mississippi governor Abram Scott. It represents the peak and the last of the Federal mansions in southwest Mississippi. Two and one half stories tall, its five-bay facade is laid with a Flemish bond brickwork, eighteen inches thick. As with the great Federal mansions of Natchez, such as

Rosalie, Arlington, and Auburn, there is a three-bay portico with towering Tuscan columns and a triangular pediment. Federal features include the semielliptical window in the pediment and the fanlighted entranceway. The original house was only one room deep on each side of a center stair hall. A rear gallery included a stair to the second level.

Local legend holds that Dr. Lynne built the house for his fiancée. She was disappointed in it, for some obscure reason, and the engagement was broken. In 1836, Lynne sold the property to Colonel John South Lewis, a Kentucky native who had immigrated to Wilkinson County soon after its formation in 1802. Colonel Lewis was one of the founders of the West Feliciana Railroad, which ran from Bayou Sara, Louisiana, to Woodville and featured the first standard gauge rails in America. Colonel Lewis's son, Captain John S. Lewis, bought the *Woodville Republican*, founded in 1824 and still published today.

The mansion remained in the Lewis family through five generations. It was bought by Holmes Sturgeon

Above: The Lewis House features a semicircular lunette. Previous page: Dr. Thomas Lynne built his Federal-style mansion for an unimpressed fiancée.

*The Lewis House has been meticulously restored after
a devastating 1998 fire.*

in 1997. A set of photos in his possession tells a story as graphic and discouraging as the old WPA pictures. Just a year after he purchased the Lewis House, a raging fire consumed the rear additions and seriously damaged the original portion. Color photos of the scene show the roof engulfed by flames and billowing clouds of angry smoke pouring from the shattered windows. Morning-after images reveal utter devastation, blackened bricks and singed columns beneath a caved-in roofline. Neighbors and friends recommended bulldozing the wreckage and consigning the Lewis House to history. The Sturgeon family was not ready to give up on the mansion, however, and slowly began the long and arduous task of reconstruction. Mounds of ashes were shoveled out, piecework was salvaged and re-created and, bit by bit, the house was brought back to life. The main front and rear doors and the elaborate ceiling medallion had, fortuitously, been in the hands of restoration artists when the fire occurred and they were carefully placed back in their original positions. Five years after the fire, the Lewis House is once again a showplace, pulled back from the brink by the dedication of the Sturgeons.

Greek Revival

Greek Revival architecture will forever be symbolically linked with the Old South in general and Mississippi in particular. But the roots of this classical style were laid sixty-five years before the state of Mississippi even existed, in a country half a world away.

Andrea Palladio's Renaissance drawings based on Roman structures were the spark for the Georgian and Adam styles of eighteenth-century England; American Federal architecture grew from those traditions. But by the mid-1700s, another ancient civilization was capturing the attention of the world. Roger G. Kennedy, former director of the Smithsonian Institution's National Museum of American History, traces the birth of Greek Revival to one expedition in the years preceding the American Revolution:

In 1751 and 1752, amid the roses of Paestum [Italy], Italian, French and English travelers suddenly recognized the presence of a complex of magnificent Doric temples. It is often said that the European Greek Revival was born in 1752, when the earl of Guilford,

who often used his courtesy title Lord North, and his friend Thomas Major measured and sketched these temples. The meticulous notes of their observations, published in a report in 1768 under the aegis of Robert Wood, became one of the most important sources of Greek Revival architecture. Wood, Major and North were eager young Hellenophiles and amateur archaeologists who went on to other things . . . In the meantime, American tourists had begun to arrive at Paestum.[9]

It's unlikely that Lord North, Thomas Major, or Robert Wood ever ventured into Mississippi. But the stir that their sketches caused would reverberate throughout the architectural world for another cen-

tury, leading to the development of a style that found some of its ultimate examples in that state.

By the 1820s, American fascination with Greek archeological discoveries had been heightened by the Greek people's war for independence from Turkey. Americans identified with the democratic ideals of the ancient city-states and were ready to turn their backs altogether on British architectural traditions. The Federal style, which had dominated American public architecture for decades, would soon give way to the newly designated Greek Revival. These buildings would be found throughout the civilized world, stretching from Russia through Europe and Great Britain and across the Atlantic to North America, but they would come to be indelibly associated with the southern states. Even though more Greek Revival structures were built and still survive in New York, Pennsylvania, and Ohio than in all the southern states combined, the later association with a romanticized Old South would link them permanently with Mississippi and her sister states of the Confederacy. In Mississippi, the domestic interpretation of Greek Revival would reach its artistic heights in houses such as Stanton Hall, Dunleith, Riverview, and Windsor. Aside from the beauty of these houses, the practicality of Greek Revival's deep porches, tall windows, and high ceilings kept the style dominant in the South long after the rest of America had moved on to Italianate and Gothic Revival homebuilding.

Greek Revival and Federal styles are often mistaken for each other, and in many ways the Greek Revival was simply a revision of the Federal. The massive porticoes and full-height columns remained, but with a twist. Federal columns were usually unadorned Tuscan cylinders. Grand houses of the Greek Revival had Doric, Ionic, or Corinthian columns made of triangular bricks that were fitted together and then stuccoed with a smooth or fluted finish. More modest houses, often built by carpenters with no overseeing architect, compromised with square columns of wood, a design never seen in antiquity. Late in the Greek Revival phase, some columns were actually octagonal. The windowed pediments of Federal styling gave way to unadorned pediments or flat-roofed porches, often stretching the full length of the facade. Cornice lines, bare on Federal houses except for an occasional line of dentil molding, were now ornamented with a wide band of trim to simulate a classical entablature. Houses built in the post-1850 era often borrowed bracketed eaves from the burgeoning Italianate style.

The Federal style's fanlighted doorways were replaced by entrances set in elaborate surrounds with rectangular transoms and sidelights. Window arrangement remained rigidly symmetrical with stone lintels a common feature.

Nationwide, the first Greek Revival buildings were public structures, just as in the development of Federal

styling. From the mid-1820s on, banks and churches and schools were invariably fronted by columns and entablatures and topped with low-pitched gabled or hipped roofs. Mississippi's Greek Revival tradition developed in a similar fashion, beginning with the Agricultural Bank on Main Street in Natchez (1833–1834). As the planned capital city of Jackson grew from a primitive backwater village to a seat of government, its landmark buildings would reflect the state's devotion to Greek Revival. The architect and builder who would leave the most enduring mark on the state's public image, William Nichols, arrived in Jackson in 1835. He took over the disastrously bungled statehouse project from John Lawrence and created the building which still stands as the Old Capitol. Over the next fifteen years, Nichols would oversee construction of the Governor's Mansion, several courthouses and schools, and the original buildings at the University of Mississippi, including the Lyceum.

Nichols was not the only architect working on memorable public projects in the state. William Gibbons was responsible for Jackson's 1846 city hall. His inability to deal with gummy Yazoo clay on the site of the Lunatic Asylum led to repeated delays and walls that crumbled almost as soon as they were erected. He was replaced by Joseph Willis, who conquered the shifting soil and built what was arguably Mississippi's most outstanding Greek Revival masterpiece, as well as the famous Madison County Courthouse in Canton.

Top: Stanton Hall's columns and capitals are world-famous. Bottom: The details of Stanton Hall represent the apex of Greek Revival opulence in Natchez.

The Irish-born Weldon Brothers employed a black draftsman, John Jackson, for their work on the Warren County and Hinds County courthouses and utilized at least one hundred other slaves who were highly trained in brickmasonry and carpentry. Mississippi's public building spree of the Greek Revival era firmly cemented its reputation as one of America's most prosperous states, with the architecture to prove it.

Domestic architecture followed the public styles. Fortunately for a later tourism industry, the peak years of Greek Revival popularity overlapped Mississippi's most sustained economic boom, roughly from 1830 to 1860. Just as the Federal style waned, Natchez and the southwest counties were hitting their stride as cotton-producing juggernauts. As cotton bales weighed down the steamboats docked at Natchez Under-the-Hill, money flowed up Silver Street to the planters and businessmen who supplied their needs. All that ready cash had to find an outlet somewhere, and in Natchez of the 1830s and 1840s, the outlet was lumber and bricks and mortar. Mansions soon lined the streets and ringed the town, each a bit grander than its predecessor. They were similar to the older Federal houses, such as Rosalie and Auburn, but differed in the significant details of columns, pediments, and cornices.

By the early 1830s, carpenters and architects were beginning to advertise their skills in the Natchez newspapers, a sure sign that trained artisans from the East Coast were migrating to where the money was. Some

were experts in their field, such as Peter Gemmell and Joseph Neibert, who built Ravenna in 1835, and T. J. Hoyt, who designed the Burn soon after. Others, often unnamed for posterity, were simply skillful carpenters with design books. They utilized Asher Benjamin's *American Builder's Companion* and Minard Lafever's *Modern Builder's Guide* to craft elaborate door surrounds and column capitals and egg-and-dart molding. Some were talented enough to reproduce these

details with remarkable accuracy; others were more limited, their handiwork just a bit out of proportion or clumsy to the untrained eye.

The early Greek Revival houses of Natchez, Woodville, and Port Gibson were not unique for long. Vicksburg was rivaling Natchez for dominance on the Mississippi River, with mansions of its own to reflect its success. With each new Indian cession treaty, more land became available in north and east Mississippi,

Dunleith is the only surviving example of "encircling columns" in Mississippi.

and settlers were pouring in to buy it at the going government rate of $1.25 an acre. Holly Springs, Macon, Columbus, Aberdeen, and Enterprise had their own cotton riches and the houses to demonstrate it. Along the Gulf Coast, New Orleans money was invested in summer homes in Pass Christian and Biloxi.

The simplicity of the basic Greek Revival design was relatively easy to duplicate in frontier towns with no trained architects. A skilled carpenter like William Turner of Oxford could fashion simple square columns, top them with an unornamented pediment and repeat the pattern with little or no alterations all over the county. Those houses would stand in stark contrast to the elaborately decorated mansions built in nearby Holly Springs by trained architect Spires Boling, with their intricate Corinthian capitals and octagonal towers.

By the late 1840s, much of America had tired of Greek Revival and moved on to Italianate styling, followed closely by Gothic Revival. But Mississippians continued to build Greek Revival mansions, occasionally incorporating Italianate brackets or window treatments or the pointed arches of Gothic Revival into a predominately Greek Revival house. As the decades passed, the mansions grew ever larger and more elaborate, culminating in an almost maniacal contest to see who could build the biggest, most expensive and ostentatious home. In Natchez, the ruins of Routh-

lands were replaced by Dunleith, with its twenty-six encircling columns and park-like setting. Simultaneously, Frederick Stanton was pouring his fortunes into Belfast, an Italianate-influenced town house that dominated an entire city block and would later be known as Stanton Hall. Downriver, James Alexander Ventress pulled carpenters from the Longwood project to transform his farmhouse into a Greek Revival/Oriental mansion. Near Port Gibson, Smith Coffee Daniell was finishing Windsor, reputedly the largest house ever in a state of architectural excess. And in Holly Springs, Salem Avenue's Montrose, Wakefield, and Athenia were rivaled only by Walter Place, a castle-like combination of Greek Revival and Gothic elements. Columbus's architectural peak was reached with the completion of Riverview and Waverley; they would be followed by a unique blend of Greek Revival, Italianate, and Gothic detailing seen nowhere else and dubbed Columbus Eclectic.

Greek Revival's longevity was attributable to several factors. Its deep porches, tall windows, and high ceilings provided natural ventilation during Mississippi's scorching summer months. The simplicity of its basic design allowed it to be duplicated in even the most remote areas. Beyond its structural advantages was an underlying psychological benefit. The people who built these mansions were demigods of their own world, with their riches and their slaves and no end in sight to

their mastery over all that they owned. A house that resembled for all the world a temple was only fitting for such lords of the realm. When the Cotton Kingdom crashed, so did the reign of Greek Revival. It would be fifteen years before Mississippians began to recover from civil war, Reconstruction, and economic and social devastation, and they would turn to newer styles and more modern fashions, leaving the Greek Revival houses as white elephants of another age.

Many of these huge mansions were abandoned as their owners moved away from agricultural pursuits; they slowly crumbled and disappeared into the encroaching vegetation. Others burned or were carved into housing for tenant farmers and sharecroppers. The huge town houses of Natchez sagged and sank into a state of chronically peeling paint and tottering columns. The epitome of the decline of the Greek Revival showplaces was Glenwood, reduced to a pathetic shell known as "Goat Castle," its fine plastered hallways and hardwood floors trampled by farm animals and its inhabitants barely able to eke out a living. It would take a stroke of marketing genius and years of work to create the pilgrimage industry that saved houses all over Mississippi. Once again, Greek Revival was revered as the symbol of a long-lost time and culture, an architectural phenomenon that reached its peak in antebellum Mississippi.

MARTHA VICK HOUSE

—Vicksburg

In 1811, the first steamboat docked beneath the bluffs at Walnut Hills, Mississippi, near the spot where the Yazoo River emptied into the Mississippi River. It was a portent of things to come, and it didn't go unnoticed by the Reverend Newit Vick, an itinerant Methodist preacher who had followed two of his brothers to the Mississippi Territory, along with his wife and a brood of children. He began buying up land in what would become Warren County, concentrating on the potentially lucrative areas along the banks of the Mississippi River.

By 1819, Reverend Vick had secured the title to eleven hundred riverside acres, most purchased for just two dollars per acre. More and more boats were pulling up to the banks there, and Vick was laying out plans for a town. Walnut Hills's population had grown rapidly in the prior decade, as had Vick's own family, which included thirteen children. Just as the lots for the proposed town were readied for sale, Reverend Vick traveled to New Orleans with his wife, Elizabeth. Both contracted yellow fever and died within days,

leaving the youngest eight children in the care of their daughter Martha.

The legal wrangling over the Vick estate continued for years. The task of fulfilling Newit Vick's dream of a riverside town finally fell to his son-in-law, John Lane. The city was laid out on a grid, stretching one block east of the river and extending eight blocks along the banks. Each Vick child drew twenty lots; seventy lots were reserved by the family to pay for various expenses. The remaining lots were auctioned off, snapped up by investors who anticipated hefty profits as cotton poured onto the docks and the steamboats lined up several deep to carry it away. Vicksburg soon surpassed Natchez as the most economically diverse and prosperous community in Mississippi.

Martha Vick was one of the older offspring of Newit and Elizabeth; as such, it was her lot to raise her siblings, as well as various nieces and nephews. She had studied at Elizabeth Female Academy in Washington, the state's first girls' school. She returned to Vicksburg, dealt with the loss of her parents, and never

found time to marry. But far from being overwhelmed by her domestic duties, she earned a reputation as one of Vicksburg's shrewdest businesswomen. She kept pace with her brother John Wesley, who owned twenty-four hundred acres of Delta land, including Anguilla Plantation, and two hundred slaves. Her cousin Henry William Vick was master of a string of plantations across Warren, Yazoo, and Madison counties and developed a popular strain of cottonseed. The Vick family was one of the most prosperous in antebellum Mississippi, and Martha was the established matriarch of the clan.

She managed her own business affairs, buying and selling property in Vicksburg and renting wharf space to steamboats, which sometimes numbered two hundred on an active day. Like the male members of the Vick family, she turned her attention and her fortune to architecture. In 1830, she built a Greek Revival town house on one of her Grove Street lots. Solid brick walls were supported by broad cypress beams. Western pine was cut in Michigan, milled in Ohio, and shipped downstream for the home. Plaster ceiling medallions and gas chandeliers were elegant touches. A separate kitchen was manned by some of the sixteen slaves Martha owned and managed.

When Martha Vick died in 1850, at the age of fifty, she willed the house, her slaves, and her fortune to younger sister Emily. Eight years later, Emily sold the house to the Methodist Episcopal Church South, which used it as a parsonage during the Civil War. It continued to serve that purpose until 1902, when it was converted back into a private residence. It has been a private home since and has been owned and preserved by Bill Longfellow and David Dabney since 1983.

The Martha Vick House was built by one of Mississippi's most successful antebellum businesswomen.

MAGNOLIA HILL

Soon after the American Revolution, brothers Samuel and Richard Swayze of New Jersey purchased almost twenty thousand acres of wilderness land along the Homochitto River south of the village of Natchez, Mississippi. They convinced fifteen families to follow them into this rugged outpost, and in 1784 Caleb King gave his name to the village of Kingston. Over the next forty years, it would be one of the most successful settlements in the Mississippi Territory, eventually claiming one hundred fifty inhabitants and several stores, a tailor, a blacksmith, and some of the first churches in the state. Farmers carved out cotton plantations and built houses to mirror their wealth. One of the finest is Magnolia Hill, sixteen miles southeast of Natchez.

Virginia doctor Alexander Boyd bought land in the Kingston area just as the community was starting to dwindle, eclipsed by Natchez and Woodville. Dr. Boyd had married the memorably named Wealthy Thomas in Tennessee before moving on to south Mississippi. At some point between 1834 and 1840 he built the house known as Magnolia Hill. It is a one-and-a-half-story rectangular frame structure with a clapboard exterior and front facade plastering. Raised on brick foundation piers, its most endearing aspect is the full-width front gallery tucked beneath an extended roofline. Box columns with no bases or capitals support the roof and are connected by balusters. Louvered jalousies extend from the ceiling to the railing top.

The interior arrangement is unusual for a classic Greek Revival planter's cottage. The front door gives entry to a large square hall rather than a stair hall; the stairway itself is tucked into a corner of the center back room. Six large rooms make up the main floor, and two windows flank a doorway at the back of the main center room. Upstairs are three bedrooms; bathrooms were a later addition. Each bedroom has a built-in closet, extremely rare for the time period in which Magnolia Hill was built.

Adding to the architectural significance of Magnolia Hill are numerous intact outbuildings. Dr. Boyd built a medical office in the rear yard, along with a schoolhouse, smokehouse, kitchen, carriage house, and cistern house. All have been restored for modern use.

Dr. Boyd died in 1866, having acquired several more plantations in Mississippi and Louisiana. His descendants lived on at Magnolia Hill until 1958, when it was sold out of the family. In 1977, it was bought by the McGehee family. Dr. Michael Wheelis acquired the house in the 1990s and has restored it fully, along with the intriguing array of outbuildings and beautifully landscaped grounds.

Following page: Magnolia Hill is an outstanding example of an early Greek Revival planter's cottage.

CEDAR GROVE

—Vicksburg

In the one hundred and forty years since the Siege of Vicksburg, the scars of that conflict have healed and largely vanished. The trenches and craters have been filled in and planted over, and the caves where Vicksburg residents huddled in misery for weeks, living on rats and mule meat, have all disappeared. The antebellum houses that survived the ordeal and the vagaries of time and economic change are pristine. But occasionally a harsh, out-of-place reminder of the city's six-week ordeal jerks the visitor back to those dark days of the Civil War. At Cedar Grove, in the midst of remarkable luxury and elegance, an angry black cannonball is lodged incongruously in the parlor wall. A Union gunboat hurled it toward Cedar Grove in the summer of 1863, where it found its target, splintering the front door and smashing through interior walls. The cannonball sailed through the house, miraculously missing the occupants, and imbedded itself in the plaster wall of the parlor. In an eccentric act of defiance by the owners, it was left exactly where it landed.

William Alexander Klein probably viewed the cannonball as a daily reminder of just how low the war had brought his fortunes. He had come to Vicksburg as a young man, around 1836, intending to make his living as a jeweler and watchmaker. Like other entrepreneurial types in 1830s Vicksburg, he quickly realized that the

real money was waiting to be made off the steamboats pulling up to the wharves. Those boats, their cargo, and their passengers had ushered in a building boom along the Mississippi River. Klein bought land near the water and put up a sawmill, churning out finished lumber for the stores, hotels, and homes that were springing up on the hillsides. His wealth grew along with Vicksburg. He invested in real estate around the booming town and opened a steam-operated compress by the riverfront. Klein's jewelry-making days were over.

By 1840, Klein was riding high and building his mansion on the eastern edge of his property. Cedar Grove, a two-and-one-half-story Greek Revival house with five bays and Tuscan porticoes front and rear, took two years to complete. The west portico looked out over the river and the east over a vast garden with serpentine walkways, ornamental animals, and a cast-iron gazebo topped with an ogee roof. After completion of the house, Klein presented it to his new bride, Elizabeth Bartley Day of Natchez. He had married well and was already enjoying Elizabeth's generous

inheritance. Twenty years later, her unique family connections would save Cedar Grove.

The Klein family grew to include ten children; as spacious as Cedar Grove was, more room was drastically needed. In 1852, a south wing was added, including a library, ballroom, and bedrooms. It was balanced in 1858 by a new north wing, encompassing a sitting room, dining room, and even more bedrooms.

This was the massive house that Union gunners sighted as they whiled away their hours on the Mississippi River in 1863. Military targets were scarce. The Warren County Courthouse, an obvious and tempting target, was known to have Union prisoners inside its walls, rendering it off-limits for practice. So the gunners turned their sights toward the mansions, which they viewed as symbols of a slaveholding society. The Porterfield house, Shamrock, suffered one hit, the missile ricocheting through the back door, down the long stair hall, and harmlessly thudding out onto the front porch. Cedar Grove also took only one direct hit, but it generated more damage. As shells rained down around the house and throughout the grounds, that one loaded charge slammed into Cedar Grove's parlor and wedged itself deep into the plaster. The Klein family escaped unharmed, but had the gunners known that Elizabeth Day Klein was a cousin of General William Tecumseh Sherman, they likely would have spared the home altogether. It was probably Sherman's influence that allowed the expectant Mrs. Klein and her children

Cedar Grove was a favorite target of Union gunboats during the siege of Vicksburg.

to escape the besieged city and seek refuge at Markham Plantation on the Big Black River. There, in September 1863, Mrs. Klein gave birth to her son, appropriately named William Tecumseh Sherman Klein.

William Klein lost his first fortune in the devastation of war. Like Vicksburg, though, he recovered quickly, founding the Vicksburg Bank in 1866 and serving as president of the newly formed Mississippi Valley Bank. Wise investments in the Vicksburg and Meridian Railroad and the Memphis and Vicksburg Railroad seeded his second fortune. By 1870 he was once again expanding Cedar Grove. A bracketed bay window, a popular Italianate feature of the time, was added to the front facade, bringing the house to its present appearance.

Six of the Klein children survived to adulthood and kept the house in the family after William Klein's death in 1884. The war baby, William Tecumseh Sherman Klein, was not one of them; as a teenager, he died of a gunshot wound while playing with a loaded rifle.

In 1919, Cedar Grove was sold to planter Antoine Tonnar. Seventeen years later it came into the possession of Dr. August J. Podesta, superintendent of Vicksburg's Charity Hospital. Over the next few decades, the mansion deteriorated and was finally abandoned. By 1960, it was in such deplorable shape, collapsing around its captive cannonball, that plans were made to demolish it and convert the site to commercial property. Fortunately, the Vicksburg Theatre Guild,

Evidence of William Alexander Klein's gardens can still be seen to the rear of Cedar Grove.

renowned for its long-running production of *Gold in the Hills*, took on the house as a preservation project and saved it. Following their restoration, it was converted into one of Mississippi's most elegant and fashionable bed-and-breakfast inns. The gardens are restored, the gazebo still boasts its unusual ogee roof, and the cannonball is preserved behind Plexiglas, a lasting reminder of Vicksburg's stormy past.

WILSON-GILRUTH HOUSE

—Yazoo City

Yazoo City was a "planned" town, a carefully laid-out development intended to maximize profits from land-hungry settlers eager to claim the rich soil along the Yazoo River basin. It was sketched in at the big bend in the Yazoo, the only spot where that river turns from the Delta to touch the loess bluffs. Excursion boats brought prospective buyers up from Natchez and Vicksburg, and the lots sold quickly. By the early 1840s, Yazoo City was a prosperous little community with businesses, churches, and fine houses lining the streets that led up from the Delta to the more healthful bluffs.

Susquehanna, Pennsylvania, jeweler Samuel Wilson somehow got wind of the opportunities to be seized in this corner of Mississippi. He moved south, purchased a lot for his house and built a large Main Street store, Wilson Hall. Planters and businessmen had money to spare in the burgeoning economy, and they must have spent much of it on jewelry and watches crafted by Wilson. His business grew, civic involvement followed, and soon he was ready to build on his residential lot. While it resembles many of the other Greek

Revival homes of the day, the Wilson House hides a unique secret. Each board was milled and numbered in Cincinnati, then shipped down the Ohio and Mississippi rivers. Smaller boats then brought the puzzle pieces of the house upriver to Yazoo City, where they were fitted together without nails. Special pegs and carefully carved woodwork were slotted together to create what *Ripley's Believe It or Not* would later dub the "first pre-fab house in America." The Wilson family moved in sometime around 1847. Their new home featured more than a dozen rooms flanking central hallways. To the rear, a detached kitchen was reached by a breezeway.

The Wilson House was a social center for Yazoo City, much as Wilson Hall came to be the gathering place for downtown merchants. At one point, the local Presbyterian membership, lacking their own building, would gather in the three parlors of the Wilson House for their Sunday services.

Yazoo City's strategic position and Confederate boatyard brought unwanted attention during the Civil

War. Federal troops destroyed the boatyard and occupied the town, marching through the residential areas in a show of strength. Young Ulysses Whitman, a Wilson family member and Confederate drummer boy, was home at the time. He stepped out on the second-floor gallery of the Wilson House to watch the soldiers march by; in willful defiance, he waved his gray cap and was shot through the arm for his efforts. For decades, the sight of the aging man with the shattered arm was a reminder of those dark days in Yazoo City history.

Samuel Wilson, never known for having a long temper, died soon after the war's end, the loser in a Main Street duel over land. His house was sold to another northerner, Colonel I. N. Gilruth, a veteran of the Union occupation who had returned to Yazoo City as a Reconstruction postmaster. As architectural fashion shifted to include more elaborate decoration, Colonel Gilruth added the elaborate "icicling" details that still outline the front facade.

In 1915, Dr. John Darrington enclosed the rear porches of the Wilson-Gilruth House and converted it

The Wilson-Gilruth House was manufactured in Ohio and shipped downriver for assembly in Yazoo City.

into a hospital. It served as Yazoo City's medical center until a new hospital was built in 1921. Since that time, it has served as a private residence, always remaining in the Gilruth family. In the 1990s, owners Cam and Byron Seward completely renovated the structure and received awards from the Mississippi Historical Society and the National Trust for Historic Preservation for the addition of a porch on the west side. The original kitchen was demolished, and one of the formal parlors was converted into a modern dining room. The house anchors the historic section of Yazoo City and has served as a stimulus for further preservation of the area.

"Icicling" woodwork was a postbellum addition to the Wilson-Gilruth House.

ROWAN OAK

Soon after the Chickasaw Indians deeded their tribal lands to the U.S. government in 1832, an Indian woman named E-Ah-Nah-Yea sold her family's section to Lafayette County pioneer John D. Martin. The wooded acreage, seemingly insignificant among the thousands of acres changing hands during this transitional period, would come to symbolize the flowering of southern literature a century later. William Faulkner walked the woods and forests of E-Ah-Nah-Yea's tribe, creating the mythical county of Yoknapatawpha.

John Martin sold his property in 1844 to Irishman Robert R. Sheegog, who had migrated to Mississippi from Tennessee a few years before that date. Sheegog and his wife had ten children, at least four of whom grew up in the house he would build in the woods. Using the simplified Greek Revival model developed by William Turner, Sheegog constructed a two-story clapboard house; four square front columns support a simple pediment and frame a second-floor balustraded balcony. A center hallway originally opened to two rooms on the right and one on the left, with a porch filling the left rear corner of the house. On the left side of the hallway, a plain stair rises and turns, leading to several upstairs bedrooms. There is no ornamentation or elaborate plastering. Sheegog also built stables, a smokehouse, servants' quarters, and a detached kitchen. Neighbor Jacob Thompson's Canadian gardener was hired to lay out the grounds, with a cedar-lined drive, magnolias, and formal flowerbeds.

Sheegog paid for all this with the proceeds from farming the six thousand acres he had accumulated in Panola, Tunica, Sunflower, and Tallahatchie counties. At the time of his death in 1860, he owned eighty-eight slaves and was one of the wealthier men in Lafayette County. His widow and four children lived on in the house through the difficult Civil War years. His youngest daughter, Mary Catherine, later related stories of Union occupation of the house and a vain attempt to hide the family silver beneath an overturned washtub in the backyard. A lucky Union soldier stumbled over the tub, knocking it aside and revealing the shallow ditch with the silver. The Sheegog house, unlike Jacob Thompson's home and much of downtown Oxford, was spared further damage during Union occupation.

After Mrs. Sheegog's death in 1871, the house was sold to Julia Bailey. Her maiden daughter, Ellen, inher-

William Faulkner bought Rowan Oak when it lacked plumbing and electricity.

ited it on her mother's death and then willed it to a sister, Sallie Bailey Bryant. Sallie Bryant lived in Coffeeville, and, rather than move back to Oxford, she rented the house out. Eighty years old and in sad disrepair, it only deteriorated further as rental property. Tenants kept dairy cattle on the grounds and plowed up much of the original landscaping for vegetable gardens. The Bryants despaired of realizing any profit from the place and put it up for sale.

William Faulkner, who just a few years before 1930 couldn't have bought the tenant house from the Bryants, much less the mansion, was in the midst of the first productive stage of his writing career. He offered the Bryants six thousand dollars with no down payment and a debt of seventy-five dollars per month. In those lean Depression times, they took the offer and accepted a deed of trust from the writer. Faulkner plunged into repair work on his own. He was driven by necessity as much as challenge, being faced with a large loan and a delapidated old house that lacked both plumbing and electricity. It needed paint, foundation work, and someone to care about it. Faulkner did, and he would live there until his death in 1962. He named the house Rowan Oak, after the Scottish symbol of good fortune.

As his career progressed, Faulkner was able to transform the house more to meet his needs. The back porch was enclosed to serve as a study or office, and that is the room where he famously scribbled the outline for *A Fable* on the plaster walls. A new porch was built off the dining room and a porte cochere added on the west side of the house. He also bought additional acreage as it came available, eventually surrounding Rowan Oak with thirty-one acres of wooded solitude.

Faulkner died in the summer of 1962, having already deeded the house and grounds to his daughter, Jill Faulkner Summers, in 1954. She in turn leased the house to the University of Mississippi for ten dollars a year, allowing her mother to stay there as much as she pleased. In addition, the Faulkners' longtime caretakers, Andrew and Christine Price, were granted rent-free occupation of their home on the property for life. After Mrs. Faulkner died in 1973, the university bought the house for $175,000 and took over its upkeep. In 1977, it was designated a National Historic Landmark, and in 1986 it was declared a Mississippi Landmark. Extensive renovations are under way on the outbuildings, and visiting scholars from around the world continue to converge on Oxford and William Faulkner's retreat in the woods.

Left: Rowan Oak's avenue of cedars was planted by Jacob Thompson's gardener.
Right: The smokehouse, tenant house, and stable at Rowan Oak were all preserved by William Faulkner.

MELROSE

The Natchez National Historical Park consists of three individual components, each representing a period of history and an aspect of the rich lore of the region. Fort Rosalie encompasses the very earliest French settlements, wiped out by enraged Natchez Indians in 1729. The William Johnson House interprets the life of a "free man of color," one of antebellum Natchez's most successful entrepreneurs and a gifted observer of human nature. The third component, Melrose, is characteristic of the planter's lifestyle in that same antebellum era. In its perfection, it is an ideal example of the Greek Revival style, which flourished in Natchez more abundantly than anywhere else.

Like most of its counterparts, Melrose was built with cotton money. John T. McMurran was a Pennsylvania native, trained in law in Ohio, who followed another aspiring young lawyer, John Anthony Quitman, to Mississippi. McMurran settled first in Port Gibson, where he taught school at Beach Hill Academy. The lure of Natchez and a partnership with the charismatic and successful Quitman were too much to resist, and McMurran moved to the bustling little city. He was soon a full partner in the law firm and handled most of the day-to-day business while Quitman played politics and fought in the Mexican War, returning home a hero.

McMurran married Mary Louisa Turner, daughter of Mississippi Supreme Court justice Edward Turner, in 1831. The wealthy Judge Turner blessed their marriage with the gift of homes at Holly Hedges and Hope Farm, along with twenty-four slaves. McMurran parlayed his legal fees and his wife's money into five plantations, totalling almost ten thousand acres and utilizing three hundred twenty-five slaves.

A man of such material success and talent, in nineteenth-century Natchez, was almost obligated to flaunt his wealth in bricks and mortar. John McMurran was no exception to that rule. In 1841, he bought a 133-acre tract of wooded land just outside the city limits of Natchez. He hired local architect Jacob Byers to design and construct Melrose, named for the Scottish abbey in Sir Walter Scott's *Lay of the Last Minstrel.* Construction of the house began around 1845 and continued for four years. While similar to many of Mississippi's other noteworthy Greek Revival mansions, Melrose achieved a degree of perfection and symmetry rarely seen even in Natchez. The nomination form for the National Register of Historic Places states the following:

In a community of magnificent mansions, Melrose is remarkable for the perfection of its design . . . though not innovative, [it] is a highly successful attempt at perfecting the Natchez plantation mansion created at Auburn and Arlington 25 or 30 years before. The dimensions are somewhat larger and the construction more solid. The Doric tetrastyle portico is modified by the broad spacing of the center columns; the iron railings are notable for their delicacy. The rear gallery is incorporated in the design and the hip roof is crowned with a balustrade.[10]

The interior spaces at Melrose are equally impressive. Rather than the usual stair hall flanked by two rooms,

Melrose, once empty for two decades, is now the centerpiece of the Natchez National Historical Park.

this house features a three-deep room arrangement with a huge foyer in the middle. The main stair is tucked into a lateral hallway. The three rooms to the right of the main entrance can be converted into one huge ballroom. Doorways are framed by Ionic columns and heavy rococo furnishings are seen throughout the house.

John and Mary Louisa McMurran moved into Melrose, along with their son and daughter, in the late 1840s. They spent most of the year there, enjoying the Natchez social whirl, and summered in Pass Christian, White Sulphur Springs, Newport, or Niagara Falls. Twenty-five house slaves maintained the mansion. Both of the children married in 1856; daughter Mary Elizabeth moved with her new husband to Maryland. John McMurran was visiting her there when Mississippi seceded from the Union in 1861. Despite his political involvement and strong Unionist sentiments, he reluctantly supported the Confederacy. His son, John, Jr., joined John Quitman's Light Artillery, one of several militia groups formed in Natchez.

The McMurrans had struggled financially through much of the 1850s. By the time of the Civil War, John had mortgaged all of his property except Melrose, and he barely hung on to it as the cotton blockade rendered his crops worthless. When Union gunboats shelled Natchez briefly in September 1862, the shells fell dangerously close to Melrose. But its location outside the lines of Union occupation meant that it was

Twin dependencies join the rear facade of Melrose, enclosing a serene courtyard.

never occupied by Union officers, as so many Natchez houses were for the duration of the war. Like many of their in-town counterparts, John and Mary Louisa befriended the Union commanders, and the Natchez party season continued as always.

By the end of the war, tragedy had struck the McMurran family, although their losses were not related to battlefields or privation. Mary Elizabeth had died and several of the McMurran grandchildren were lost to the frequent childhood diseases of the time. Searching for peace of mind and a change of scenery, McMurran sold Melrose to another lawyer, George Malin Davis, in 1865. The McMurrans planned to relocate to Maryland to be closer to their son-in-law and surviving grandchildren. But before they could move, McMurran booked passage on the steamboat *Fashion* for a quick business trip to New Orleans. It was an ill-fated decision. Cotton stored on the boat caught fire near Baton Rouge, and dozens of passengers were killed as the *Fashion* sank. John McMurran managed to swim ashore but died a few days later of his injuries. Mary Louisa never left Natchez, moving instead to her parents' home, Woodlands, where she lived another twenty-six years.

The new owner of Melrose, George Davis, had one child, Julia, who married New York doctor Stephen Kelly. When Julia died, Dr. Kelly moved back to his native state with their only son, George Malin Davis Kelly. Melrose was left fully furnished but unoccupied for twenty years.

In 1901, young George Malin Davis Kelly and his new bride came south to Natchez to inspect their property there. By a fortuitous combination of marriages and intermarriages, the young man had inherited four of Natchez's most significant mansions when he was just eight years old. Choctaw, Cherokee, Concord, and Melrose were his for the choosing. Concord, once the home of the Spanish governor of Natchez, burned soon after his arrival in the region. With three left to select from, the Kellys decided on long-empty Melrose as their home. After two decades of neglect, it was not an inspiring sight: "The walls dripped water by the bucketful; a few of the carpets had rotted, and several draperies had been eaten by moths. Wooden doors warped so badly that some could not be opened; dead birds and small animals had fallen down the chimney. Yet all the furniture, the paintings, the fluted

columns were there. Melrose had waited."[11] The furnishings, draperies, and painted floorcloths were the originals picked out almost sixty years before by John and Mary Louisa McMurran. They had been sold, along with the house, to George Kelly's grandfather and passed down intact through the family. By the odd coincidence of several generations with only one child in each, the land and furnishings were never split among siblings, leaving this as one of the few intact estates in Natchez.

The Kellys restored and maintained Melrose, living together there until George's death in 1945. Mrs. Kelly, the young New York bride brought south to face the overwhelming task of managing four antebellum mansions, lived on at Melrose until 1975. In 1988, Congress created the Natchez National Historical Park. Two years later, Melrose was purchased from the Kelly estate as a fitting centerpiece for that park. The National Park Service now maintains it as one of their premier properties, opening its doors to thousands of national and international visitors every year.

BEAUVOIR

—Biloxi

Beauvoir is the quintessential Mississippi Gulf Coast planter's cottage: facing the water, it is surrounded by deep verandas and is perfectly situated to catch every breeze from the Gulf of Mexico. Even in the modern era, with four lanes of Highway 90 just a few feet south of the lawn, its idyllic setting is evident. Originally called Orange Grove, the house was built as a summer retreat, later served as a writer's sanctuary, and for decades provided a peaceful hideaway for aging veterans.

Madison County planter James Brown chose the site for his family's coastal cottage in the mid-1840s, purchasing the property from Pass Christian developer John Henderson. The house was constructed sometime between 1848 and 1852. It had to be spacious; Brown and his wife had eleven children. A sawmill was erected on the grounds and lumber cut right from the yard. Brown served as his own architect and contractor, bringing in skilled laborers from New Orleans to do the interior decorating.

The main house is a square block encircled by deep porches. An unusual glass-paned front door opens

into a wide central hallway with two main rooms on either side. Two projecting wings extend off the rear. Mrs. N. D. Deupree described the house in 1903:

It is a large and commodious home, with a frontage of sixty feet and a depth of seventy feet. It stands in the center of an enclosure five hundred by seven hundred feet. It fronts the south and the sea, where the placid waters roll lazily over the white sands or the great waves chased by the storm king break over the beach with the sound of distant thunder. Twenty-five broad steps lead up to the wide verandas which extend along three sides of the house. The veranda roof is supported by huge fluted columns. The whole structure is upheld by brick pillars. The entrance is made through folding doors with wide glass panels. A hall sixteen feet wide extends through the house from south to north. On the left of the entrance are the parlors, dining-room, and the family sitting-room; on the right are the bedrooms and nursery; this was the arrangement when it was the home of

Left: Beauvoir's shutters have weathered a number of hurricanes.
Right: Beauvoir was the sanctuary where Jefferson Davis penned his memoirs.

Mr. Brown and family. The rooms are all large, and high-ceiled, with two long wide windows in each. Generous fire-places attest that even beside the summer sea a fire is sometimes necessary.[12]

Flanking the house are two small cottages, one designed originally as a schoolhouse and office, the other as a home for circuit-riding preachers.

The Brown family used the house only as a summer retreat, and after Mr. Brown's death in the late 1860s, it was sold to Frank Johnston. He, in turn, sold it almost immediately to Sarah Ellis Dorsey. Mrs. Dorsey was the stepdaughter of Charles Dahlgren, the builder of Dunleith in Natchez, and she maintained her primary home in New Orleans. Sarah had grown up with Varina Howell, Jefferson Davis's second wife. She was

educated in England and dabbled in writing, turning out several novels and magazine articles.

Jefferson Davis's fortunes in the postwar period had been dismal. He had failed at several business ventures, had spent time in Europe, and was facing an old age of poverty and defeat. He was also increasingly obsessed with writing his memoirs, in hopes of documenting the brief history of the Confederacy and his role in its heyday and demise. In 1876, his nomadic existence led him to New Orleans, where he was introduced (or possibly reintroduced) to Varina's lifelong friend, Sarah Dorsey. She immediately offered Davis the use of her beachfront home for his writing retreat. He gratefully took her up on the offer, although he insisted on paying her fifty dollars a month for rent. One of the small cottages was renovated to provide writing space and a bedroom, and Davis set to work on *The Rise and Fall of the Confederate Government* and *A Short History of the Confederate States*.

Varina Davis was furious with the arrangement. She remained in England, refusing to move to the Coast with Davis and fuming at Sarah Dorsey's efforts to encourage Davis's writing. It would be several years before Varina finally consented to move to the Coast and be with her husband. Sarah was dying by the time Varina arrived, and she offered to give the house to Davis outright in her will. A clause was inserted so that no one would mistake her intentions:

Varina Howell Davis stipulated that Beauvoir would be a Confederate soldiers home and shrine to her husband.

I owe no obligation of any sort whatever to any relative of my own. I have done all I could for them . . . I therefore give and bequeath all my property, real, personal, and mixed . . . to my most honored and exteemed [sic] friend, Jefferson Davis, ex-president of the Confederate States, for his sole use and, in fee simple forever; and I hereby consitute him my sole heir, executive, and administrator. If Jefferson Davis should not survive me, I give all that I have bequeathed to him to his youngest daughter, Varina. I do not intend to share in the ingratitude of my country towards the man, who is in my eyes, the highest and noblest in existence.[13]

Holding to the remnants of his pride, Jefferson Davis made several payments to Sarah Dorsey's estate to purchase Beauvoir. Even before his death in 1889, it was being transformed into a shrine, attracting admirers and old soldiers who adored their former leader and came to pay him homage. Davis left the house and grounds to his daughter, Winnie. She wrote three novels while living there and died in 1898. Beauvoir then passed into the hands of Varina Howell Davis, who turned down a hotel developer's offer of ninety thousand dollars for the property. In 1903, she sold it to the Sons of Confederate Veterans for ten thousand dollars, stipulating that it be converted to a Confederate soldiers' home and a shrine to her husband. When Mrs. Deupree visited soon afterwards, she found it to be a sad sight. "Beauvoir ceased to be a home; and, as turn by turn the wheel of time goes on, the old home is slowly sinking into the sere and yellow leaf. Let us hope the sons and daughters of those who followed the mandate of the Southern chieftain will restore it to its pristine beauty; and let it be done quickly."[14]

The Sons of Confederate Veterans lost no time in opening the Jefferson Davis Soldiers' Home on the property. The operation was soon assumed by the state of Mississippi, and the house and outbuildings were quickly bursting with old warriors and their dependents. Twelve dormitories, two hospitals, a chapel, and dining and asssembly halls were constructed to handle the overflow. For the next forty years, the veterans would while away their declining days on the broad porches of Beauvoir. More than seven hundred were buried in the Confederate Cemetery behind Beauvoir. As their numbers dwindled, the reunions and battle tales became scarcer. A 1926 photo shows a group of feeble men, most with crutches or wheelchairs and some with a leg or an arm missing, proudly arrayed in front of their leader's last home.

By 1956, there were no more veterans to roam the halls of Beauvoir. Gradually, the dormitories disappeared and the main house was converted into a museum. Fifty-seven acres of the original estate remain, surrounding what is now known as the Jefferson Davis Shrine.

THE MAGNOLIAS

Aberdeen grew up along the Tombigbee River in the 1840s, one of the earliest and most successful towns of northeast Mississippi. Its architecture reflects the prosperity of those antebellum years in the numerous mansions and planter's cottages scattered throughout the town, as well as the later period of opulence represented by the Victorian houses of "Silk Stocking Row."

One of the finest houses of Aberdeen's antebellum period is owned by the city itself. The Magnolias was built by Dr. William Alfred Sykes, one of three Virginia brothers who ventured into the Aberdeen area in its earliest days. Sykes built the Magnolias for his wife, who lived only a year after its completion in 1850. In its symmetry and setting among huge, ancient magnolia trees, the house is like a Hollywood set piece of the Old South. Frazer Smith, who oversaw renovation of the house in the 1930s, described the effect in *White Pillars*:

From the street the approach is through an avenue of dense, low-hanging magnolia trees which close off the house entirely except for an occasional white spot when the wind is blowing and shifting the leaves. Sun spots sift through the foliage to find a brick here and there on the broad aged brick walk partly covered with moss and ivy creeper. The facade, when close enough to be seen, presents six square pillars of Doric origin, springing from a first floor level seven feet off the ground and extending through the entire height to the roof line, creating a gallery of unusual charm and comfort. The other facades present white wood walls penetrated by well framed fenestration with dark green shutters.[15]

The interior of the Magnolias features the usual central hallway with two rooms, upstairs and down, flanking the hall on either side. The staircase is the truly unique creation in this house. A mahogany stair rises from the front of the hall, as does a black walnut stair from the rear. The two meet in the middle of the hallway, cross and rise to a landing, then split again to reach the second floor. Frazer Smith stated that he had seen this arrangement in only one other house, Cunningham Plantation near Cherokee, Alabama, but an almost identical stair is found in Aberdeen's Holliday Haven.

The Magnolias remained in the Sykes family for five generations, owned last by Corinne Sykes Acker. It was purchased by Clarence D. Day II in 1985 and presented to the city of Aberdeen as a memorial to his parents. Carefully maintained and preserved, it is used for receptions and special events and opens each year during the Aberdeen Pilgrimage.

The Magnolias was a gift to the city of Aberdeen from the Day family.

RIVERVIEW

The Tombigbee River prairie's rich soil was a magnet for settlers even before Mississippi became a state. Some of the earliest communities, such as Cotton Gin Port, were short-lived. But by the 1820s, Columbus was a thriving river town, one which would soon rival far-off Natchez in economic and architectural ascendancy. And, as in Natchez, the tendency of wealthy planters to build homes in town with their cotton fortunes would leave a legacy of mansions and grandeur which is still evident a century and a half later.

Charles McLaran came to Columbus from Baltimore in the 1830s and made a fine living in cotton production. Along with other successful planters and businessmen, he founded the First National Bank of Columbus. By 1850, he was listed in the census as the second-largest landowner in Lowndes County. Like most of his planter/businessman/professional counterparts, he chose a site within the city limits of Columbus on which to build the inevitable mansion.

McLaran could not have escaped familiarity with the work of architect James Lull, whose projects dominated

both public and private architecture in Columbus through its most prosperous years. Lull's own home, Camellia Place, was the epitome of Greek Revival styling, solid and symmetrical and eye-catching. McLaran bought an estate-sized lot overlooking the Tombigbee and contracted with Lull to reproduce Camellia Place, only on a grander and even more ornate scale. Perhaps Lull was flattered, or perhaps he was distressed at the prospect of his own beautiful home being overshadowed by the newer home; his

response to the request has been lost to history. Nevertheless, Lull worked on Riverview from 1847 until 1853. Local interest, even in this community of exceptional homes, was high, and the local paper ran an article to describe the house in its November 12, 1852, issue:

Our townsman, Col. Charles McLaran, recently had erected on one of the most eligible and beautiful situations within the limits of our city, a splendid and costly brick mansion, the crowning architectural structure among the many stately edifices, private and public that adorn our city, and delight the eye of the stranger en passant, *and which, in dimensions and external grandeur, internal arrangements, style and exquisit [sic] finish is, probably, superior to anything of the kind to be found in the Southern States. [The house] includes an entire square in the plan of the city, bordering on the bank of the Bigby river on one side, and is enclosed by a neat pilastered brick wall about five feet in height, except the entire front and a small space in the centre of the rear, where a*

Left: Riverview's grounds originally occupied an entire city block in Columbus, overlooking the Tombigbee River. Right: Riverview is one of Mississippi's most elaborate Greek Revival mansions.

Two spacious porticoes placed exactly opposite, the one in front and the other in the rear, each supported by four insulated antae, standing in rows parallel with the walls of the building, and rising from marble plinths up to the eaves of the main structure, with pavements composed of the most exquisite marble mosaic work, complete the outlines of this stately private residence.

Inside the house, pilaster walled parlors, adorned with the richest entablatures—spacious party saloons, and private boudoirs—*mantles of the purest Egyptian marble,—ceilings of the most lofty elevation, the richest plaster panel work, and the most superb finish,—an admirably contrived and elaborately executed spiral stairway—a chef d'ouvre [sic] in this art—starting from the centre of the building on the first floor, and terminating at the observatory—comprise a few of the most striking objects which present themselves on all sides.[16]*

highly ornamental cast-iron paling supplies its place, and gives an air to the premises alike tasteful and imposing. The building occupies a central position in the square, surrounded by luxurient [sic] native forest trees, and is a solid quadrangular figure, of the Corinthian or composite order, constructed of the finest compressed brick, wrought into plastered walls, covering an area sixty one feet square, and rising forty feet in height from the base to the eves [sic]; surmounted by an observatory, twenty feet square, and towering up to an elevation of sixty feet above the ground, the spacious windows of which, three on each side, by the cunning contrivance of the artist, present to the eye of the observer from within, the appearance in the surrounding objects of the four seasons, viz. Winter, Spring, Summer and Fall.

The two-and-one-half-story red brick mansion retains most of the details described in that 1852 article. Its St. Louis–manufactured bricks are laid in an all-stretcher veneer, and the entire structure exhibits the most rigid symmetry. Brick pilasters with marble capitals and bases subdivide each facade into five equal bays; where the exterior chimneys would interfere with the spacing, a false window is placed with closed shutters to simulate an opening. The east and

The spiral stair in Riverview soars from the ground floor to the cupola.

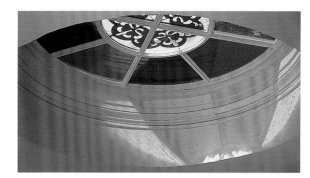

west facades have identical full-height porticoes, supported with the square stuccoed brick pillars found throughout Columbus. The porticoes are floored with marble and surrounded by cast-iron railings.

The low-pitched hip roof is covered with the original slate and topped with a large square cupola. The cupola has three windows on each side, glazed in red, cobalt, green, and amethyst glass to simulate the changing seasons.

On the interior, a sweeping spiral stair extends from the main floor up to the cupola. It begins in a large stair hall which separates the three rooms on each side. On the south, double parlors are divided by a panel which can slide up into a second-floor space, making one large room. On the second floor is a large ballroom and several bedrooms. Throughout are elegantly carved ceiling medallions, mantels, and pilasters.

Colonel McLaran and his family lived in Riverview until 1857, when it was sold to hotelier John Gilmer. Like all of Columbus's mansions, it survived the Civil War without serious threat, and in 1881 it was sold to W. W. Humphries. The Humphries family and their descendants lived there until the 1960s. By that time, the old house had deteriorated to the point where demolition or conversion to commercial use was almost a certainty. Luckily, Frances Thomas lived across the street. Her efforts to salvage this icon of Columbus culture eventually led to her purchase of the house and the beginning of restoration. In 1971, she sold the home to Dr. and Mrs. John Murfee, who restored it to its original glory. In 2001, it became only the thirty-fifth site in Mississippi to be designated a National Historic Landmark.

Left: Each side of Riverview's square cupola features three windows, glazed in colors to represent the seasons.
Right: Riverview's stair curves into a domed cupola, flooded with light.

TULLIS-TOLEDANO MANOR

—Biloxi

The fortunes and families of the Mississippi Gulf Coast are inextricably entwined with those of New Orleans. A strong French influence is reflected in the names and traditions of the region, and much of the original development of Mississippi's coast was linked to New Orleanians' desire for the sea breezes, live oaks, and ambiance of their neighbors to the east. Pass Christian and Ocean Springs were originally resort communities; Biloxi and Bay St. Louis reflect both the architecture and the romance of the Crescent City.

In 1856, Christoval Sebastian Toledano, a hugely successful cotton and sugarcane broker in New Orleans, traveled to Biloxi in search of a new wife, having recently been widowed. He was a guest at the famous Green Oaks Hotel, one of the region's earliest luxury hostelries and possibly its first gambling hall. The proprietor's daughter, Matilde Pradat, thirty years Toledano's junior, caught his eye. Within months they were married and making plans to build on the lot next to the Green Oaks. The view over the Mississippi Sound was breathtaking, and Toledano was deter-mined to build his new bride a house worthy of the setting.

The house that Christoval Toledano built for Matilde, designed and supervised by her uncle, Jean Marie Pradat, is a graceful two-and-a-half-story block of red brick with upper and lower galleries looking out over the shoreline. It's not an especially spacious house, with a large hallway serving as one room, flanked by two more rooms of equal size and two smaller ones attached to the rear. In one of the rear spaces, a spiral stair leads to the upstairs rooms. In the French tradition, often seen in the West Indies and the earliest houses of Natchez, the primary access to the upstairs is an ornate turning stair on the east end of the front gallery. Six brick Tuscan columns support the gallery on the first floor, tapering into chamfered tim-ber posts on the upstairs gallery. The columns are sunk several feet into the ground, probably in anticipation of hurricanes. The orientation of the house maximizes the Gulf view and captures the cool breezes across the galleries. Inside, high ceilings and floor-to-ceiling win-dows serve as a natural air conditioning system. Each window is bordered by heavy cypress shutters hooked on with the original iron fasteners.

On the interior, Mr. Toledano commissioned French painter Jules LeGrande to craft elaborate murals on the walls and ceilings. The paintings were often described as unusual, even eerie, with scenes of veiled and bonneted women, obese men, and cos-tumed hunters.

Christoval and Matilde Toledano raised their three children in the house. Toledano died there in 1870, leav-ing the house and twenty-eight acres to Matilde. She stayed on until 1886, selling the property that year to her niece, Carmen Valle, for twenty-one hundred dollars. It stayed in the family until 1906, when it was sold to Dr. Thomas Osborne Hunter for forty-five hundred dollars. Just a year later, he sold it to his sister-in-law, Mrs. Vin-nie Philbrick, at a one-thousand-dollar profit. Mrs. Philbrick took an immediate dislike to the strange murals. The moldy, peeling plaster was unsightly and smelly as well, so she simply had the walls replastered, in

The Tullis-Toledano Manor has survived hurricanes, fortune hunters, and neglect to become a favorite Gulf Coast attraction.

the process erasing all traces of the murals. Her nephew recalled the paintings that he had studied as a child: "One of the things that I remember about the house was when I was a small boy and use [*sic*] to lay on my back in the living room and look up at the ceiling on which was painted faces—some smiling, some sad, and some looked insane. When my father sold the house to my aunt, Vinnie Philbrick, she thought the paintings were old, faded, and of no account and covered them with fresh plaster."[17] Mrs. Philbrick also modernized the house, enclosing space on the back gallery for a kitchen and adding plumbing and electricity.

The house stayed in the Philbrick family until they lost it during the Great Depression. John B. Campbell bought it at bank auction and then sold it, in 1939, to Jules A. Schwan. A year later, it finally found an owner who appreciated its antebellum charm. Garner H. Tullis was, ironically, a New Orleans cotton broker, just as Christoval Toledano had been, and president of the New Orleans Cotton Exchange. He acquired the manor as a summer home, came to love it, and spent decades restoring and preserving it.

Three years after Garner Tullis's death, the Tullis-Toledano Manor was battered by Hurricane Camille. The original outside stair was ripped away and the interior suffered considerable damage. Floodwaters crept five feet up the plastered walls. The future of the unique old house seemed bleak.

Mrs. Tullis sold the property to the city of Biloxi in 1975. It has been carefully restored and maintained as a house museum. Visitors are told of the gold piece that Matilde Pradat's younger sister hid in the foundation as the home was being built in the late 1850s. This story may have given rise to legends that Christoval Toledano hid his fortune in jars buried beneath the lawn. Several of the outbuildings have disappeared over the years, victims of treasure hunters. An even more pernicious threat to the house has been the encroachment of casinos across Highway 90. But in the midst of the neon, noise, and rushing traffic, the Tullis-Toledano Manor endures, an oasis of elegance in the midst of another century.

ATHENIA

—Holly Springs

In her 1950 history of Holly Springs, Olga Reed Pruitt anointed Athenia (then called the Clapp-Fant House) "The House of Great Men," an homage to the remarkable line of legislators, judges, generals, and businessmen who had lived there. She could have just as readily called its location, Salem Road, "The Street of Great Houses," for it is lined with several of Mississippi's most outstanding architectural achievements. Airliewood and Cedarhurst are perhaps the finest extant Gothic structures in the state; Montrose, Wakefield, and the lost Pointer Mansion exhibit the apex of Greek Revival detailing. But none of these homes surpasses Athenia in its pure classicism and wealth of ornamentation.

The 1840s found Holly Springs in the midst of one of its periodic economic booms. The courthouse square was bustling with lawyers and merchants, and a new moneymaking venture was capturing the attention of men with excess capital to invest. The Mississippi Central Railroad sprang from the imagination of a group of Holly Springs visionaries, and its completion lured even more money into the prosperous town.

Jeremiah W. Clapp wisely invested in that railroad, and its profits added to his income from a busy law practice. He split his time among Holly Springs, Jackson, where he served as a state legislator, and Oxford, where he sat on the board of trustees for the new University of Mississippi.

Judge Clapp tapped his railroad earnings, his law practice, and his wife's considerable family fortunes to finance the Greek Revival mansion on Salem Road,

replacing a frame house which had been built on the lot in the previous decade. In a town that was rapidly becoming renowned for its architectural achievements, the Clapp house was rivaled in elegance only by Walter Place. Fifty years after it was built, it still inspired glowing description:

It is an old colonial mansion, set far back in a grove of stately oaks, many of them luxuriantly draped in ivy . . . Judge J. W. Clapp, who superintended the construction so carefully that it is said he saw every brick and piece of timber that went into the structure. If a workman ever succeeded in slyly putting an imperfect brick or piece of timber in, he only made double work for himself, for he surely had to take it out . . . The hall is unusually spacious and opens into rooms of almost lordly dimensions. The double parlors and library are each twenty feet square, with ceilings eighteen feet high. On each side of the folding doors between the parlors, there are fluted columns reaching from floor to ceiling. The walls are

Confederate relics were found in the capitals of Athenia in the 1940s.

ornamented with rich cornices done in fleur-de-lis *with borders of Greek key-work; the mantels are of marble exquisitely carved in grapes and leaves. The dining room at the end of the hall is oval in shape, thirty feet long, lighted by four long windows which open on the gardens and lawns . . . A broad curving stairway, adorned with statuary in niches placed at intervals, leads to the second story hall of the same dimensions as the one on the first floor.*[18]

Judge Clapp, admired statewide for his rhetorical skills, was elected to the Confederate Congress in 1861. It was a logical honor, but one that would come back to hound him as the war consumed Holly Springs. The town reeled back and forth from Union to Confederate occupation for several years. Judge Clapp's prominence in Confederate politics rendered him a prize target for Union apprehension; twice he barely evaded capture by troops. He recorded his first narrow escape in his diary:

> *I took refuge in the house of a near neighbor, Mr. Nelson, who helped me up into the loft and covered the entrance with a piece of furniture. The day was warm and the heat of my hiding place almost unendurable, but upon reflection I concluded that it was more tolerable than a Yankee prison and submitted to the roasting until the danger was over.*[19]

A few months later, Judge Clapp endured an even more harrowing escapade:

> *I was still in bed [when] my son Will came dashing into the room with the exclamation—'The Yankees are in the yard and have got Beck [Judge Clapp's mule]!' Of course I lost no time in getting out of bed,*

but what to do next was the question. My clothes were on a chair at the bed side, but I had no time to put them on. A servant girl stuck my boots up the chimney and put my watch in her bosom and my wife disposed in some way of my hat and clothes, and as I could not venture outside, I made my way to the attic or garrett in my night apparel, and in

Left: Athenia is one of several landmark Greek Revival homes on Holly Springs' Salem Road.
Right: The columns of Athenia provided an unusual hiding place for Judge Clapp.

looking anxiously about for a hiding place it occurred to me to get inside of one of the large iron capitals that finished the columns to my front porch. Here I was completely concealed, but could hear the Yankees riding on the pavement in the front yard and talking, and supposing they knew I was at home and had come on purpose to capture me, and would set the house on fire if I did not make my appearance, my feelings at the time may be better imagined than described. Will, however, very adroitly managed to get rid of them and save Beck, and I was after awhile able to leave my place of concealment.[20]

A haunting reminder of this tale surfaced almost eighty years later, when a pistol holder, saddlebags, and a cartridge case stamped "CSA arsenal" were found in the Corinthian capital during attic renovations at Athenia.

Union officers were quartered throughout Holly Springs's mansions, including Athenia, when General Earl Van Dorn staged his famous dawn raid on Holly Springs on December 20, 1862. The pandemonium on Salem Road was described by an eyewitness: "Out of the house the Yankees came tumbling, rushing through the yard, down the lane, over the orchard fence, on into the woods they went half clad, as it was just daybreak."[21] The Confederates wreaked almost as much havoc as the Union forces had done, but for the

moment Holly Springs was back in sympathetic hands, however briefly.

Judge Clapp wearied of his life on the run and moved on to Memphis, where his son would one day be elected mayor. Athenia was purchased by another remarkable gentleman, General Absalom Madden West. Madden West was an Alabama native, founder of the Attala County town that bears his name, and an admired legislator and Whig partisan. He vigorously opposed secession; failing to stop it, he offered his services to Mississippi when war came. He was appointed a brigadier general and also filled the positions of quartermaster general, paymaster general, and commissary general. As the war wound down, he took the dubious position of president of the devastated Mississippi Central Railroad and moved to Holly Springs to oversee its revival. The once-powerful railroad had borne the brunt of Union fury when troops swept through north and central Mississippi. Rails were torn apart, heated to plasticity, and wrapped around tree trunks as "Confederate necklaces." Even the engine named for General West, the A. M. West, was wrecked in a head-on collision with the James Brown near Duck Hill, Mississippi, with thirty Confederate soldiers lost in the accident. Railcars were wrecked and burned, and the scanty remaining stock bumped along the splintered tracks and stretches of

open land, often as not pulled by mule power rather than engines.

General West moved into Athenia and set to work rebuilding his railroad and his state. Undaunted by the challenges facing him, he scoured the state for financing, manpower, and materials. The Mississippi Central would be absorbed in the 1880s by the Illinois Central system, but by then West's reputation as an innovative and resourceful leader was already secure. He turned his talents again to politics and was a stabilizing influence through the dark years of Reconstruction. He was nominated for vice president by the National Party in 1880 and by the Anti-Monopoly Party in 1884. When he was home at Athenia, he tended dozens of acres of orchards, fruit trees, and flowers. One of his children married Judge Clapp's daughter; another married the granddaughter of Choctaw chief Greenwood Leflore, and yet another son was engaged to a daughter of Supreme Court justice L. Q. C. Lamar, but died before the marriage.

Madden West died in 1893 and was buried in Hill Crest Cemetery. The house was bought by Lester Glenn Fant, a lawyer and jurist who served as United States attorney. His son, Glenn Fant, Jr., was a judge for many years in Marshall County. Athenia is now owned by Dr. and Mrs. Ben Martin, Jr., and is undergoing a complete and faithful renovation.

STRAWBERRY PLAINS

—Holly Springs

Strawberry Plains is possibly the most ideally located plantation in Mississippi. Reaching it requires driving for quite a distance off the main highway, over deep ravines and gullies, into a world of thick underbrush, ancient trees, and total silence except for birdcalls and the rustling of forest wildlife. It's one of the few places in the state that would be recognizable to the pioneers who first claimed this land from the Indians in the 1830s, before the woods were cleared and the fields planted. The house itself stands in a small clearing in the midst of the twenty-five-hundred-acre preserve, surrounded by avenues of cedar trees that radiate away from the house like spokes in a wheel.

The fact that Strawberry Plains still exists is a testament to three women. One stood her ground against all odds in defending her home and family; the other two, a century later, saved that home and its unusual setting for generations to come.

Ebenezer Nelms Davis, a successful planter with several thousand acres and more than one hundred slaves, built Strawberry Plains in 1851. He had married

the indomitable Martha Greenlee of Virginia and built the two-story brick house with four fluted columns for her and their six children. The interior arrangement was the usual "four up and four down" combination of formal rooms and bedrooms. The Davises were benevolent slaveowners by the standards of the day, defying Mississippi law and local taboos to educate their workers and provide them with their own church.

Although the house site seems isolated now, in 1861 it was on one of the main roads to Holly Springs. This proximity would bring the war right to the front doors of Strawberry Plains. As Union troops approached Holly Springs in 1862, marauders invaded the house and severely beat Ebenezer Davis. Family lore relates that they mistakenly assumed a relationship to Jefferson Davis, despite his protestations to the contrary. For his own safety, Davis went to Alabama, leaving Martha and the children alone at Strawberry Plains.

Even with Ebenezer gone, tragedy and hardship dogged the Davis family. As Marshall County see-sawed between Confederate and Union occupation,

foragers ranged freely through the fields and forests of the plantation. Martha encountered one Union soldier raiding her smokehouse; when confronted, he cursed her. She pulled a pistol from her skirts and fatally shot him. It didn't take long for word to reach his commanding officer, who questioned Mrs. Davis on her actions. When informed that the soldier had used foul language, the officer commended her and went on his way. She continued to defy Federal constraints by running the blockade on household goods, slipping away with neighbor Eliza Stephenson to Memphis to bring back necessities.

Before the war left north Mississippi, Strawberry Plains was set afire by Union troops. Martha's entire household was ill with chicken pox. Considering her reputation for self-preservation, it's a wonder she didn't single-handedly fight off the soldiers, but she was forced out of her home with the whole brood. Much of the home's interior was destroyed, but the brick shell of the house was salvaged. When the war ended, the Davises managed to refurbish two rooms,

and it was in that environment that they lived and raised their children.

The house was still largely a ruin when Thomas Finley acquired it sixty years later. It would be another forty years before his daughter, Margaret Finley Shackleford, and her husband, Dr. John Shackleford, renovated it in the 1960s. They added the first indoor plumbing and electricity and restored the original rooms. A beautiful curving stair from a Memphis Shriners' hospital was dismantled, numbered by pieces, and reassembled in the main hallway.

Margaret Shackleford and her sister, Ruth Finley, bequeathed the Audubon Society, Marshall County, and all of Mississippi a priceless treasure in 1983. Milton Winter describes their decision in his book *Shadow of a Mighty Rock*:

Acting out of deeply felt beliefs, on January 8, 1983, Dr. John W. and Mrs. Margaret Finley Shackleford, with her sister Miss Ruth Finley, gave property including two thousand acres of land and two magnificent antebellum homes to the National Audubon Society, a memorial to Thomas Finley, longtime clerk of session in the Holly Springs church, and his wife, Mrs. Ruth Leach Finley. The gift included "Strawberry Plains," a large plantation with an impressively restored Greek Revival mansion, erected in 1851, generally regarded as the most beautifully sited antebellum plantation house in North Missis-

sippi . . . Situated several miles northwest of Holly Springs, "Strawberry Plains"—much of it planted in forests such as once covered North Mississippi—was deeded for the purpose of forming a wilderness sanctuary for native birds and animal species.[22]

The Audubon Society has carefully maintained the house and a nearby sharecropper's cabin, now used as a visitors' center. The woods have grown up again

around the house and provided just what the Finley sisters intended, a glorious preserve for wildlife and their family home. A varied program of educational and wildlife conservation projects is planned for the future, but the centerpiece of the concern will always be the restored mansion. The strength of Martha Davis and the generosity of the Finley sisters are immortalized in its walls.

Left: Avenues of ancient cedars radiate from Strawberry Plains like spokes of a wheel.
Right: For decades, Strawberry Plains was little more than a burned-out shell.

BELMONT

An antebellum house in the Mississippi Delta is a rare sight. This rich land, which would prosper during the Cotton Kingdom's second stage in the late 1800s, was sparsely populated in the years before the Civil War. Without levees to hold back the annual spring floods from the Yazoo, Tallahatchie, and Sunflower rivers and myriad streams and creeks, it was uninhabitable. Vast cypress swamps were roamed by bears and choked with alligators and water moccasins. Those few pioneers adventurous or foolish enough to try their hand in this harsh land battled malaria, typhoid, and yellow fever. It was much easier, and immeasurably safer, to plant cotton in the gentle hills of Marshall County or along the Tombigbee River prairies than to risk life, limb, and fortune in the Delta.

There was one exception. On the very westernmost edge of the region, Washington County was a remote outpost of pre–Civil War civilization. Greenville grew into a decent-sized town in the mid-1800s, and a hardy contingent of Kentuckians and Carolinians carved out plantations along the banks of Lake Washington. Set-tlements with names like Wayside, Chatham, Erwin, and Glen Allen ringed the lake and gave rise to most of the Delta's rare antebellum architecture.

The sale of Choctaw Indian lands in the 1820s and Chickasaw lands a decade later brought an influx of settlers to north and central Mississippi. Only a few were willing to tackle the challenges of the Delta, with its heat, floods, fevers, and wild animals. Of those who did, none made a more lasting architectural impact than the Worthington brothers. Kentucky natives Samuel, Elisha, William, and Isaac Worthington bought thousands of acres of land in Mississippi and Arkansas and established vast plantations. Each brother built at least one house. Isaac's was Leota, close by the Mississippi River at Leota Landing. He ignored the warnings of his neighbors that the house was too close to the river. Rising spring floodwaters took first his lawn, then swept Leota from its foundations and off to the Gulf of Mexico. Samuel Worthington's Wayside was a thirty-eight-room mansion that also, if more indirectly, was a flood victim. It withstood the disas-trous 1927 holocaust, only to be condemned and demolished when the new levee construction placed it on the west side of the earthworks.

Of all the Worthington houses, only Belmont remains. The land where it stands was sold by the U.S. government to Governor Alexander G. McNutt, the first white man to own it. Samuel Worthington purchased it in 1853 to complement his three existing plantations: Redleaf, Mosswood, and Wayside. Two years later Samuel sold it to his brother, Dr. William W. Worthington. Worthington was apparently more of a planter than a doctor, as evidenced by his eighty slaves and the hundreds of acres which surrounded Belmont. He built his house between 1855 and 1861. It is a blend of the prevailing Greek Revival and Italianate styles of the day. The main two-story block is red brick with a full-height portico featuring square Doric columns, turned balustrades, and a pediment pierced by a circular window. The cornice line is heavily bracketed. The roof is of shallow pitch, hipped and crowned with molded chimneys. Windows are tall and

Belmont is the only one of four Worthington homes to survive in Washington County.

narrow, capped with stone lintels. An ell extends from the main block to the rear.

Inside, Belmont features some of the finest decorative plaster work in Mississippi. Local lore holds that German plaster artists were stranded in Washington County when the Civil War started; having no means of escape and no other work, they whiled away the war years carving intricate molding and ceiling medallions into Belmont's plaster. Another version relates that Dr. Worthington met a group of Italian carvers on a boat trip to New Orleans and convinced them to return with him to Belmont. Regardless of its origins, the decorative work in Belmont rivals the finest interiors of Natchez or Columbus.

The large central hall is backed by an elegantly turned stair. Two rooms open on either side of the hallway. To the right, the formal rooms can be divided by huge wooden doors which glide in and out of the walls. On the left are two bedrooms. Upstairs are four more bedrooms, separated by a wide hallway that serves as a sitting room. Ceilings soar to fourteen feet

on both levels. A two-story ell adds several more bedrooms, kitchen space, and offices, all opening onto long, high-ceilinged screen porches that look out over endless cotton fields. Altogether, the house encompasses nine thousand square feet, with three thousand square feet of porch space, ten bedrooms, and nine fireplaces.

Originally, the grounds extended to the Mississippi River. Just across the road (now Highway 1) was Wayside, the home of Dr. Worthington's brother, Samuel. That house suffered more directly than did Belmont during the Civil War, with one of Samuel's sons being shot by Union soldiers in his own pasture. Roving bands of troops wreaked havoc across Washington County for several months, foraging and burning Greenville. Remarkably, all of the Lake Washington homes, including Belmont, were spared.

Belmont remained in the Worthington family until the early 1930s. A young girl living at Wayside in the early years of the twentieth century recalled Dr. Worthington's son, always known as "Mr. Will":

"[He] was really a southern gentleman. He wore white linen suits and panama hats and on hot days he carried a parasol, or umbrella, and he was a very genteel person."[23]

Governor Dennis Murphree bought the house from the Worthington heirs during the Depression and converted it into a hunting lodge. Over the next half-century, it was occupied only by hunters and sportsmen. The elegant rooms were filled with bunk beds, mattresses, muddy boots, and deer heads. Plaster cracked, and sections of the elaborate ceiling medallions crumbled. A room in the back ell was designated for drinking, in a valiant effort to keep inebriated sportsmen from further damaging the old home. After the hunting club disbanded, Belmont was converted back into a private residence. Mr. and Mrs. Fernando Cuquet have restored it to its antebellum elegance. It stands a few hundred feet back from the traffic of Highway 1 as a last reminder of the Worthington brothers and the pioneers who claimed the Delta.

For decades, Belmont's rooms housed only a hunting club.

MOSBY HOME

—Canton

Canton is a town of intriguingly varied architecture, both domestic and commercial. It boasts one of the most picturesque and economically vibrant courthouse squares in Mississippi, and its residential streets radiate off that square at shaded angles. The architectural styles vary from the stark solidity of the Shackleford House to the exuberant gingerbread, corner towers, and wraparound porches of the late Victorian era. But the most visually dominant house is, without question, the Mosby Home, an eyepopping mansion rising at the end of Lyon Street.

It is an established fact that Colonel Wiley Lyons arranged for the construction of the house that rises over the street bearing his name. The year is less of a certainty, with sources estimating anywhere from 1846 to 1856. The Mississippi Department of Archives and History lists the date of construction as circa 1852. Regardless of the date, Colonel Lyons's creation is a massive main square of red brick, five bays wide, dominated by a full-height portico and four columns topped with Egyptian capitals. Rising from the roof is a tall belvedere with arched windows on each side. A

deep dry moat surrounds the house and gives access to a basement level. Two wings extend off the rear, forming a U-shaped courtyard.

The premier feature of the Mosby Home's interior is its staircase. The stair hall is twenty feet by forty feet, large enough to balance the soaring curve of the walnut stair. It seems to float out of the hallway as it disappears into the upper floor. At that level, a more tightly corkscrewed stair rises on to the cupola. Legend relates that Colonel Lyons left for Europe without specifically directing his architect to build the stair from the ground floor to the cupola; when he returned, the main stair was complete and there was no access to the cupola. The error was rectified with the addition of the smaller staircase.

There are ten thousand square feet under the roof of the Mosby Home. The main rooms are twenty feet by twenty feet with fourteen-foot ceilings.

Colonel Lyons suffered reverses during the Civil War and never actually finished the house. He sold it to W. J. Mosby in the 1870s, and it has remained in the family since that time.

Left: Wiley Lyons incorporated a vast array of details into his Canton home.
Right: The Mosby family has owned this Greek Revival showplace for several generations.

DUNLEITH

—Natchez

In a town known worldwide as the repository of America's Greek Revival showplaces, Dunleith represents the ultimate expression of that style. Twenty-six stuccoed brick columns completely encircle the square structure, supporting an elaborate entablature and a hipped roof with multiple chimneys and six dormers. Only a handful of peripteral (completely encircled by columns) houses were ever built; fewer still survive. Columns of the Forest and Windsor are all that remain of those homes in Mississippi. Forks of Cypress in north Alabama burned just a few years ago. Nothing remains of Louisiana's Uncle Sam Plantation except a mounted bell. Near St. Francisville, Greenwood has been faithfully reproduced after the original house was destroyed by fire in 1960.

Hidden behind the massive bulk of Dunleith, well back on its rolling estate grounds, are reminders of a house known as Routhlands. Routhlands was one of the earliest fine homes of Natchez, dating back to the first decades of the 1800s. It was enlarged and modernized by Job Routh, who added a second story,

columns, and galleries. More intriguingly, he also built a collection of outbuildings in the Gothic style, several of which survive. The garage/kennel is topped with a turreted hexagonal columbary. A two-story brick barn is fronted by a wooden carriage ramp and ground-level stable; the roof is outlined with a crenallated parapet. A greenhouse and a servant's lodge with Tudor gable ends are also still extant on the terraced lawns behind Dunleith. The highest level of the terraces is reached by fifteen stucco steps with flanking bases and urns. These steps may have been the main approach to Routhlands.

Routhlands was the home of Job Routh's son and daughter-in-law and their four children. When the younger Routh died, his widow, Mary Ellis Routh, married Charles Dahlgren, a hot-tempered businessman who had come to Natchez after a successful banking career in Philadelphia. Dahlgren frequently bragged of the knife scars and pistol balls he carried on his body, but he was readily accepted by Natchez society upon his marriage to Mary Ellis Routh. In addition

to her four children, they would have seven sons of their own, and the combined family lived at the Routhlands estate until it burned in 1855. Dahlgren blamed his wife's whimsy for the fire: "[It] was struck by lightning and destroyed, in consequence of my wife desiring terra cotta chimney tops placed, which were elevated above the surrounding china trees, and so affording an object for the electric fluid."[24]

It was a fortunate day for Greek Revival architecture when Routhlands burned. Dahlgren hired John Crothers to build a house which would come to symbolize the apex of that style, ideally situated in all its glory in the midst of the forty-acre estate. Completed in 1856, the new Routhlands, as the Dahlgrens continued to call it, is a massive two-and-one-half-story cube with colossal Tuscan columns extending around every facade, connected by ornamental galleries on both upper and lower levels. Brackets beneath the cornice are closely spaced, and the hipped roof is pierced by dormers and chimneys. The house originally had a rectangular cupola, long since removed.

Dunleith is built on the site of Routhlands, a Natchez mansion predating statehood.

The interior features the typical wide stair hall with two rooms on either side, characteristic of the late Greek Revival period. Elaborate ceiling medallions, chair rails, and marble mantels complement the classical woodwork throughout. Windows can be raised a full six feet, offering access to the breezes from the galleries. Additional heat relief was afforded by fifteen-foot ceilings. Joined to the rear of the mansion is a three-story, eighteen-room servants' wing. Inside it and extending beneath the main house are the remnants of a rare nineteenth-century plumbing and heating system.

Mary Ellis Routh Dahlgren lived in the house only two years before her death. Charles Dahlgren had no intention of staying on without her. Within a month of her death, he had placed an ad in the local newspaper: "For sale. My residence Routhlands, including 50 acres of land. Apply on premises. C. G. Dahlgren."[25]

The house sold quickly, bringing Dahlgren and his stepchildren thirty thousand dollars. New owner Alfred Vidal Davis moved in and renamed the house Dunleith. He would soon sell it to Hiram Baldwin, who in turn sold it to Joseph Carpenter. It remained in the Carpenter family for five generations. It is now owned by the Worley family and functions as a bed-and-breakfast, a wedding venue, and an instantly recognizable symbol of Natchez.

The Gothic outbuildings that served Routhlands are a stark contrast to the Greek Revival Dunleith.

NEILSON-CULLEY-LEWIS HOUSE

—Oxford

Merchant William Neilson moved to the frontier village of Oxford in 1836 and set up a general merchandise store in a crude log building. A few years later Oxford attracted young William Turner, a self-taught architect/builder from North Carolina. Neilson's name would come to symbolize the finest in clothing stores for several generations; Turner would leave an equally impressive architectural legacy that, in its own simplistic manner, rivaled the best of Natchez, Holly Springs, and Columbus.

By the late 1850s, Neilson had worked his way to success, and, like his contemporaries who profited from cotton, he was ready to build a town house. William Turner had built many of those homes, fashioning a unique style from which he rarely deviated. The Sheegogs, Carters, Shipps, and several other families had contracted with Turner to build two-story frame Greek Revival structures. Each featured one or two full-height porches with four square, unadorned columns, lacking plinths and capitals. Wrought-iron balconies were centered above the main entrance.

Inside, the primary doorway would open onto a long center hallway, often crossed by a shorter one toward the rear, forming a Maltese cross. Spacious, high-ceilinged dining rooms, parlors, libraries, and bedrooms were included. Ornamentation was minimal, or in some cases, absent altogether.

The Neilson house was centered on a sloping hillside, several blocks southwest of the square. William Neilson planted an avenue of cedar trees leading up the incline from the street to the house. They lead to the primary portico, which is mirrored by an identical structure on the north side of the house.

When war came, Neilson paid to outfit a Confederate unit and joined a local militia company. Union officers commandeered his house during the occupation of Oxford in 1862; they must have been treated well, for this was one of the few homes spared when General A. J. "Whiskey" Smith's troops laid waste to Oxford in August 1864. All but one building on the square was destroyed, as were several of Oxford's largest houses. What remained was described by an eyewitness as "the most completely demolished town they have seen anywhere."[26] The mansion belonging to the former Secretary of the Interior Jacob Thompson was torched, as was Thomas Pegues's Edgecomb. The former vanished in flame, but Edgecomb was salvaged by the timely arrival of Confederate troops. The Neilson House, the Sheegog House, and the Carter House were fortunately untouched.

Most antebellum homes in Oxford feature paired square columns.

The tragedy of war did not completely bypass the Neilson House. A true incident was fictionalized by Stark Young in his novel *So Red the Rose.* As Federal troops paraded through conquered Oxford, five-year-old Ed Neilson and a black playmate clambered into a tree on the front lawn of his house, hoping to watch the soldiers undetected. One of those soldiers broke ranks, drew a bead on the children, and killed the servant boy with one shot.

Ed Neilson carried the memory of that horrible incident throughout his life and may have personally related it to fellow Oxonian Stark Young. In the 1890s he rebuilt Neilson's Store on the new square and saw it through another generation of service. His maiden sisters, affectionately known to locals as Miss Anna and Miss Lou, stayed on in the aging mansion and supported themselves by giving china-painting classes in an upstairs bedroom. After their deaths, the home was owned for many years by Dr. John Culley and his wife, Nina Somerville Culley, who updated and enlarged the mansion.

Despite some hard years, the Neilson House fared better than its identical twin, the Carter-Tate House, which gradually caved in on itself, its haunting hallways attracting generations of Ole Miss students fascinated by the peeling plaster and rotting floorboards. William Faulkner's vivid descriptions of southern architectural decline may have been inspired by that doomed structure. Although the Neilson House never deteriorated physically, its looming presence may have been the setting for Faulkner's eerie short story "A Rose for Emily." Faulkner's own home was very similar to the Carter-Tate and Neilson houses and was also built by William Turner.

Over the course of the past century, the Neilson-Culley-Lewis House has passed through several families, including the Morses and the Adamses, who altered the stair from its original straight simplicity into a graceful turned curve, opening up the hallway to serve as another room. Ironically, the house now belongs once again to the owners of Neilson's, Will and Patty Lewis. Their side yard fountain is encircled by bricks from the long-destroyed Lafayette County Courthouse, salvaged by a sheriff almost 150 years ago. William Neilson's towering cedars still line the front sidewalk, leading forever to the classical portico that has witnessed so much of Oxford's history.

William Turner built several Lafayette County houses, all with two-story porticoes and scarce embellishments.

STANTON HALL

The road to riches in antebellum Natchez nearly always ran through some aspect of cotton production. Planters were the most obvious beneficiaries of the endless demand for cotton fiber; many doctors and lawyers and businessmen forsook their claimed profession as soon as they accumulated enough land and slaves to declare themselves "gentlemen farmers." Frederick Stanton made his fortune in a slightly different manner, brokering cotton. He took the finished product from someone else's fields and arranged to have it sold, shipped, and delivered to New Orleans, always taking his own cut. If there was a "clean" side to the cotton kingdom, Stanton had found it, and his success would be mirrored in the same manner as that of the planters and the gentlemen farmers. As the glory days of Natchez neared their end, Stanton was building the house that is considered by many to be the ultimate achievement in Mississippi's antebellum architecture.

Combining Greek Revival and Italianate elements, Stanton Hall is grander and more ostentatious than

almost any house in town, although it was completed only a few months before Stanton died and a few years before the Civil War doomed it to "white elephant" status. A Natchez writer summed up Stanton Hall's fate: "Here stood the ultimate exhibit of the cotton era. Overblown, almost over-ornate, Belfast [the original name] was like the ripe red rose that bears within itself the seeds of decay. The days of simplicity had ended. Belfast appeared to sum up the last tense days of the Deep South, when planters, as if in defiance of

an impending doom, were piling elaboration upon elaboration."[27] The story of Stanton Hall is the story of the peak, decline, and rebirth of Natchez as the symbol of the Old South.

As a young man, Frederick Stanton had immigrated to Natchez from Ireland, along with two equally successful brothers. He realized the profits to be made in brokering the torrents of cotton flowing out of southwest Mississippi, and by the 1830s he had accumulated enough of a fortune to buy his first mansion, Cherokee. He lost the house in the Panic of 1837 but quickly regrouped and bought it back. Along with his wife, Hulda, a Natchez native, he was ready to build his dream house by 1851. He chose a high city block in downtown Natchez and set about designing the ultimate home in a city of mansions. His name for the house would be Belfast, in honor of his Irish roots.

Englishman Thomas Rose went to work on Belfast in 1851; it would not be complete until 1857, a date immortalized in the plaster of the pediment. Both exterior and interior elements were above and beyond

Left: Architect Thomas Rose carved the date "1857" into Stanton Hall's pediment.
Right: Frederick Stanton spent years planning and building Belfast, only to die within months of its completion.

anything seen before in Natchez. Rising high above street level, the four giant order fluted columns are joined by lacy iron railings at each level. Corinthian capitals top the columns. The hip roof is capped with a huge, arched-window belvedere. Inside, a seventy-five-foot-long hallway features fifteen-foot ceilings, its enormity broken only by an elliptical arch mounted on consoles. Doorways are framed with heavy Greek Revival ornamentation. To the right of the main entrance, a music room and ballroom are joined by sliding doors, creating a seventy-two-foot-long promenade. The impression of even greater length is achieved by the reflections in the tall pier mirrors at each end. Across the main hallway, a library and formal dining room are separated by a stair hall, its mahogany stair curving from the main level to the third-floor attic. On the second floor, six bedrooms open off another huge hallway. A service wing runs off the back of the house. Marble mantels are placed throughout the formal rooms and bedchambers.

Stanton had planned the house in his mind for years. As it rose into reality, he headed for Europe on a buying spree, shopping for appropriate furnishings and ornaments to fill the vast rooms. He had to charter a boat to bring back the moldings, wrought iron, chandeliers, mirrors, and furniture he had custom-ordered. The family moved into Belfast in 1857. But within three months, Frederick Stanton was dead, and Hulda Stanton was left with a veritable castle to maintain.

The family stayed in Belfast through the Civil War, despite occupation of the upstairs bedrooms by Union officers and the theft of the family silver. They held on through Reconstruction, but, by 1894, they could no longer maintain the huge home. It was sold to a group of educators to serve as Stanton College for Young Ladies. The women's school occupied it until 1901, when the students and teachers moved to Choctaw. Stanton Hall passed through a series of owners over the next thirty years. At one point, it was so undervalued and unwanted that it sold for less than the original price of its wrought-iron fencing. By the onset of the Depression, the future of Stanton Hall, as it had come to be known, was bleak. All over Natchez, the aging symbols of the Cotton Kingdom were sagging and neglected. Several burned, others were torn down for lack of funds to refurbish them, and one, Glen-wood, slid into a state of such degradation that it came to be nationally known as "Goat Castle." Stanton Hall was just one more money pit with no future.

An act of nature and the dogged determination of Natchez matrons saved the great house and its neighbors. A late freeze and wilted azalea blooms led a frantic group of ladies to open their time-weathered mansions as an alternative to the annual garden show. The response was overwhelming. Over the next decade, busloads of "pilgrims" poured into Natchez, creating a crucial funding source for the salvation and maintenance of the town's historic homes. Realizing that Stanton Hall was never likely to serve as a private home again, the members of the Pilgrimage Garden Club voted to buy it and restore it for future generations. In the years since, their careful attention to detail and authenticity have revived Stanton Hall, probably the most photographed and well known of all the Natchez houses. Frederick Stanton's dream was, as described in a National Register of Historic Places nomination form, always "more successful as a showplace than a residence."[28] The thousands of visitors who tour it each year would agree.

Stanton Hall is lavishly embellished with Greek Revival and Italianate ornamentation.

Italianate

After the strict classicism of the Federal and Greek Revival periods, Americans turned to Italianate architecture in the 1840s. The style had emerged in England as a reaction to two centuries of Palladian, Georgian, and Greek Revival strictures. It took its inspiration from the farmhouses and country villas of Italy, incorporating the arched windows, bracketed eaves, and towers of those homes. Its major proponent in the United States, Andrew Jackson Downing, stressed the harmony between the built and the natural environment in his 1850 *Architecture of Country Houses.* His drawings emphasized deep eaves with single or paired brackets, narrow round-arched windows with crowns or inverted U-shaped molds, and square towers or cupolas, often soaring to three stories.

Italianate architecture enjoyed an extended period of popularity in Mississippi, resulting in some of the most extraordinary homes of the antebellum and postbellum eras. Two of the landmark examples were lost to fire. Annandale was a three-story, forty-room mansion in Mannsdale, west of Madison. It was completed

in 1859 and later described by a descendant of its owner, Margaret Johnstone:

The completed product contained forty finished rooms on three floors. Only two rooms were finished on the third floor. No expense was spared in decorating the mansion. The plaster work was done by special artisans and the cornice moldings were deep and ornately designed . . . Ceilings on the first floor were sixteen feet high, fourteen feet high on the second floor, and twelve feet on the third floor. The great hall was entered through massive double doors with an enormous fan-light transom above . . . The great hall was twenty-four feet wide by about eighty feet in length. At the end of this hall a staircase rose to a

landing and then branched out to the right and left to ascend to the second floor. The fact that the end of the hall was circular made the branching staircase spiral in appearance . . . The entire house was built of long leaf pine and cypress and would, I am sure, be standing and in excellent condition today if it had not burned on September 9, 1924.[29]

Margaret Johnstone's daughter and son-in-law built the other grand Italianate mansion of Madison County. Ingleside was an extended one-story house with long arched loggias and a central tower. It burned in 1906.

All told, relatively few Italianate mansions were built in Mississippi, though the Vicksburg area does claim a significant number of postwar Italianate cottages and town houses. The curves, brackets, and towers of Italianate styling made these homes technically more difficult to construct, especially for carpenters working from pattern books. Their complexity made them more expensive to build, and their irregular floor plans were not as conducive to air flow and cooling as were Greek Revival plans. Italianate *features* did gain a large degree of popularity as an adjunct to Greek Revival; by the late antebellum era, bracketed eaves were appearing on mansions like Stanton Hall and Edgewood in Natchez, Swiftwater in Washington County, and the Mosby Home in Canton. Bay windows were added to older Greek Revival houses such as Cedar Grove in Vicksburg.

Of the antebellum Italianate houses that have survived, two are true mansions with numerous unique features, and three are towered villas that mirror the work of A. J. Downing. Ammadelle is a landmark home in Oxford, designed by Calvert Vaux, the architect of New York's Central Park. Vaux's signed drawings remain in the house, which was nearly destroyed by Union soldiers in 1864. Its irregular massing, bracketed eaves, window hoods, rounded archways, and elaborate chimneys are all elements of Italianate styling. Nearly two hundred miles away, on the shores of Lake Washington, Mount Holly stands as a near mirror-image duplicate of Ammadelle. Many of the features are similar, but the overall quality of Mount Holly's construction is not equal to that of Ammadelle.

The three towered antebellum Italianate houses which are extant in Mississippi are Wohlden, Rosedale, and the Boddie Mansion at Tougaloo. Both Wohlden and Rosedale boast impressive center towers with paired windows incorporated into the facade of the main house. The Boddie Mansion has a separate roof tower which soars above the main block of the structure. All have the rounded arches and brackets characteristic of Italianate architecture.

Had the Civil War not intervened, the Italianate style might have become more prevalent in Mississippi. The 1860s and early 1870s passed the state by in an architectural sense. More stable regions of the country during that era indulged in an elaborate version, referred to as High Victorian Italianate. Mississippi's rare exposure to that style was evident only in areas that bounced back from Reconstruction quickly, such as Columbus, Aberdeen, and Natchez. When widespread stability returned to Mississippi, the Italianate era had been eclipsed in favor of the Stick and Queen Anne styles, whose features are seen in many of the existing late-1800s houses throughout the state.

Italianate style uses elaborate towers and arches.

ROSEDALE

One of the most popular architects of the mid-nineteenth century was Andrew Jackson Downing, whose design books promoted the harmony of the natural environment with the human habitat. In his most famous book, *The Architecture of Country Houses*, Downing defined what he considered to be the ultimate home, a "country villa":

That home in the country which is something beyond a cottage or a farm-house, rises but to the dignity of a villa or mansion. And this word villa—the same in Latin, Italian, Spanish, and English signifies only "a country home or abode;" or, according to others, "a rural or country seat"—as village means a small collection of houses in the country. More strictly speaking, what we mean by a villa, in the United States, is the country house of a person of competence or wealth sufficient to build and maintain it with some taste and elegance . . . The villa, or country house proper, then is the most refined home of America—

the home of its most leisurely and educated class of citizens. Nature and art both lend it their happiest influence. Amid the serenity and peace of sylvan scenes, surrounded by the perennial freshness of nature, enriched without and within by objects of universal beauty and interest—objects that touch the heart and awaken the understanding—it is in such houses that we should look for the happiest social and moral development of our people.[30]

Four true "Italian villas" from the antebellum era are extant in Mississippi. Only one, Rosedale, remains in its intended pastoral setting. Rosedale is probably not a Downing design; it bears a striking resemblance to "Design Six" in Samuel Sloan's 1852 *Model Architect*, another popular style book of the day. Sloan also waxed eloquent on the attributes of the Italian villa:

Country residences in the Italian style are becoming more and more popular, both here and in the old world. Its great pliability of design, its facile adaptation to our wants and habits, together with its finished, elegant and picturesque appearance, give it precedence over every other. It speaks of the inhabitant as a man of wealth, who wishes in a quiet way to enjoy his wealth. It speaks of him as a person of educated and refined tastes, who can appreciate the beautiful both in art and nature; who, accustomed to all the ease and luxury of a city life, is now enjoying the more pure and elevating pleasures of the country.[31]

Rosedale's porch is framed by flattened arches.

W. W. Topp may have thought of himself in exactly these terms. He bought land south of Columbus from Emily Craven in 1853 and soon after began building his villa. The setting was just what Downing and Sloan would have chosen: a considerable but not impractical distance from town, surrounded by meadows and pastureland. Topp was a land speculator who settled in Columbus and became a planter of considerable means. The 1850 census lists him as a man of fifty years, married to Otezia and claiming four children. He was a member of St. Paul's Episcopal Church and was respected enough in the community to receive an appointment to the board of the Columbus Female Institute.

Topp's Rosedale is a classic Italian villa, an eye-catching surprise in a broad park-like meadow. It is two stories of stuccoed brick with an imposing three-story square tower in the center of the main facade. The hip roof is extremely low-pitched and appears to be almost flat when seen from a distance. The foundation is raised and scored to resemble stone; attractive iron ventilators are spaced along the base. At the base of the tower is a full-length porch outlined with carved woodwork. On the tower, a canopied balcony is enclosed by a cast-iron balustrade. Round-arched windows and bracketed eaves complete the Italianate detailing of the house.

On the interior, the main hall is fourteen feet wide and separated from the vestibule by a semicircular molded arch. A winding stair with mahogany railing winds up from the hallway. Two rooms open off the hallways on each floor. Separate stairs from the second floor lead into the tower.

Samuel Sloan's plan was almost certainly the basis for the creation of Rosedale, but it is not known if he was directly involved in the building of this house. He had commissions in Woodville, Natchez, and Tuscaloosa during the period of Rosedale's construction, but no correspondence or contracts exist to tie him to Columbus. A worn copy of *Sloan's Constructive Architecture: Guide to the Practical Builder and Mechanic* was found in the attic of another Columbus house, lending credence to the theory that a local builder may have borrowed liberally from Sloan's design and technique books, a common practice of the time.

Today, Rosedale's square tower soars above the rolling pastureland that surrounds the house. Heavy Natchez rockers line the front porch, whose ceiling is painted a calming blue shade. Architectural curators are at work on the house, utilizing time-honored methods and modern computers to determine the original wall colors and wood-graining techniques. When their work is complete, Rosedale will, as much as possible, be identical to the "country villa" that W. W. Topp knew as home.

W. W. Topp's Rosedale is a prime example of the pastoral Italianate villa.

WOHLDEN

—Canton

On a quiet street just off the famous Canton square, Wohlden is tucked behind azalea bushes and gates topped with cannonballs salvaged from the Vicksburg battlefields. Its central tower bursts up through the trees, marking it as one of the state's most outstanding examples of Italianate architecture. To the casual eye, it appears to be a creation of the 1850s, fashioned at the height of the Italianate style's popularity in the decade before the Civil War. But hidden deep within Wohlden are traces of a much older house, a primitive dogtrot, one of the first houses to grace Center Street soon after the founding of Canton. And while the present-day gardens and brick walkways are works of beauty, they are just the last remnants of a nationally renowned horticultural paradise.

Colonel David Matthew Fulton left Baltimore for newly created Madison County in the early 1830s. He built a simple two-room dogtrot cabin in the recently platted town of Canton, heating the rooms with corner fireplaces and cooling them with a central breezeway and a front gallery. Fulton was a cotton planter

who quickly profited from his operations in the rich Big Black River bottom. Over a twenty-year span, he acquired fifty slaves, employing them in cotton production and running his ferryboat back and forth on the Big Black. His wealth allowed him to enlarge and improve his dogtrot house, the alterations probably being done in the early 1850s. The front gallery was converted into a hallway and another long, high-ceilinged hall met it at a right angle. Two formal par-

lors were added on either side of the main hall, and elaborate ceiling medallions and dentil molding framed those rooms. Heavy chandeliers hung throughout and a carved wood stair rose out of the main hall. It led to an upstairs hall which gave entrance to several bedrooms. A small curved stair rose into the most distinctive feature of the house, the central tower.

That tower is the dominant feature of the Italianate style which David Fulton utilized for the transformation of his house. Its vertical mass dominates the front facade; the two main blocks of the home are fronted by a one-story gallery wrapping around both corners, supported by simple box columns. A pediment over the main entrance is topped by the tower with its paired windows, louvered shutters, and cast-iron grating. A "captain's walk" and gold ball crown the tower. Two stuccoed, corbeled chimneys break the roofline.

Colonel Fulton had only a few years to fully enjoy his expanded and improved home. Madison County was economically ravaged by the Civil War, as was the colonel. Papers found in his desk in the 1950s show

Left: Inlaid square bricks of Wohlden's walkways
Right: The Italianate facade of Wohlden hides an older dogtrot house incorporated into the floor plan.

had for many years been surrounded by large boxwoods, perhaps planted by Colonel Fulton, and the Ruckers added camellias, hydrangeas, and jasmine to transform the old home place into a massive, elaborate garden. Pergolas and square brick walkways wound through the colorful grounds. By 1936, the abundance of foliage attracted the notice of *Holland's Magazine,* which sent a writer south to tour the gardens:

In Spring the garden is stimulating with the sheer abundance of its glorious color, intoxicating with the perfume of jasmine and Regal lilies. The pageant of iris and columbine, larkspur and poppies, pentstemon and Canterbury-bells passes. Later is a gorgeous show of perennial phlox. As the heat of summer begins to be felt, pastel shades predominate in the garden. Shasta daisies, white periwinkle, scabiosa and petunias, white and primrose, Phlox drummondi—cooling and refreshing by day, fairylike and luminous under the summer moon. Zinnias, dahlias, cosmos, and pompon chrysanthemums bring the season to a close.[32]

"Miss Maria" Rucker faithfully tended her gardens until her death in 1940. Just a few years later, blight destroyed the boxwoods, and the entire garden gradually vanished. Mrs. Ben Johnson, affectionately known to her Canton neighbors as "Miss Solie," took over care of the family home and lived there until her

that the house was confiscated by the federal government and that Colonel Fulton actually had to pay rent, to the tune of twenty dollars for two weeks, to the Freedmen's Bureau. This indignity entitled him to remain in his own home. Fulton received his pardon from President Andrew Johnson in October 1865, and his property was then restored to him. His fortune was

gone, however, and he was shipping only one-tenth of his prewar cotton production.

When both Colonel Fulton and his wife perished in an 1878 yellow fever epidemic, the house passed down to their descendants. By the 1920s, it was in the hands of a grandniece and grandnephew, Edward and Maria Rucker, both blessed with green thumbs. The house

Cannonballs from the Vicksburg battlefield crown the gateposts of Wohlden.

death. She was chatting with a visiting Jehovah's Witness one day when they decided to pry open Colonel Fulton's plantation desk drawer, frozen shut since his death. That effort yielded a treasure trove of antebellum letters and records, reflecting the prosperity of the prewar years and the struggles through Reconstruction and the late 1800s.

In 1967, Collins and Sis Wohner bought the house and contracted with Yazoo City architect Jack DeCell to update and modernize the home. It is surrounded by the original cistern house, kitchen, and barn. Next door is a tiny Greek Revival office building, only two rooms deep, but stunning in its detail and temple-form perfection. It originally stood in Sharon, but was moved to Canton in the 1850s, where it served as a dental office. Later owners used it as a girls' school, a music studio, and even, according to local legend, as an office for Dr. Tichenor, inventor of the enduring antiseptic. The Wohners saved it from destruction and now divide their time between these two outstanding examples of Mississippi's architectural legacy.

This two-room Greek Revival temple has served as a school, music studio, dental office, and medical office.

BODDIE MANSION

In 1869, two former Union generals found themselves back in Mississippi, wrangling over a piece of land and a house which just a few years before they might have destroyed. The house was the Boddie Mansion, and the land would form the nucleus of one of America's premier black educational institutions, Tougaloo College.

John Williams Boddie was one of many sons born to a rich planter in North Carolina. With sixteen siblings and half siblings, he was not likely to inherit much in his native state, so he followed four of his brothers to Mississippi. The five Boddie brothers accumulated land near Jackson and in Madison and Coahoma counties. John chose acreage straddling the border between Hinds and Madison counties, near the railroad crossing of Tougaloo Station, and it was there that he began building his Italianate mansion in the 1850s.

Local stories and family lore differ on John Williams Boddie. Some tales claim that he was building this two-story frame house, complete with its commanding belvedere, for a fiancée who wanted to be

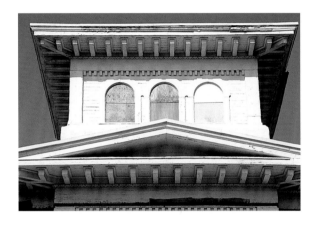

able to see her native Jackson. She never married Mr. Boddie and never lived in the house, but the reason is uncertain. One story relates that she jilted him, another that she simply died before the wedding. Another legend tells that the dejected Boddie refused to live in the house and used it for hay and cotton storage. That tale is refuted by the family's proof that displaced members of the Boddie clan moved into the mansion after their own home was destroyed in General Sherman's sweep through Jackson.

The ultimate truth of John Boddie's romantic disappointments and disposition of his house may never be known, but it is documented that the Boddie Mansion was constructed by master builder Jacob Larmour. He was also the architect of Mississippi College's Provine Chapel, Grace Episcopal Church in Canton, and Margaret Johnstone's landmark Italianate house, Annandale. Larmour utilized Hinkle, Guild & Company of Cincinnati to supply the millwork and other elements of the Boddie Mansion; the finished house is illustrated on page fifty-four of the 1862 edition of that company's catalog, listed as "Residence of J. W. Boddie, Madison County, Miss; J. Larmour, Architect and Superintendent, Canton, Mississippi."[33] The drawing shows the house as it was originally designed, with a three-bay facade and projecting central pavilion with an open pediment. An arched gallery runs across the front elevation, and two smaller porches are found on each side of the house. The windows are round-arched and the front entrance doorway is capped by a semicircular fanlight. The eaves are

Left: Legends say John Boddie built this tower for the fiancée who jilted him.
Right: The Boddie Mansion is being restored to its original elegance by Tougaloo College.

very deep and bracketed, and the entire structure is capped by a soaring belvedere with arched windows on each side. John Boddie died before the Civil War ended. His will, dated November 3, 1863, is interesting in its detail: "I desire to be interred in a metallic coffin without show or parade by the side of my brother in the graveyard in Jackson. I give all my estate both real and personal . . . to my nephews, sons of my brothers . . . I give $1000 to each of my nephews . . . $500 to my nieces . . . I give my Negro men Joab and Corry and my woman Cesi $10.00 every year and recommend them good treatment."[34]

Boddie's estate was forced to sell the house and its accompanying acreage in the late 1860s. The American Missionary Association, a benevolent group established to aid and educate freedmen, was searching for a location to build a normal and agricultural school for former slaves. They dispatched retired Union general Allen Huggins to find a site in central Mississippi. Huggins was familiar with the huge house and land at Tougaloo, but before he could buy it, it was snapped up by another Union officer, George McKee. McKee's intentions were not especially philanthropic; he planned to subdivide the land and sell it to freedmen. The two old soldiers waged an acrimonious battle over the land before Huggins finally arranged for the AMA to purchase the Boddie Mansion and five hundred acres for $10,500.

Tougaloo Normal and Manual Training School opened in the Boddie Mansion in 1869, headed by H. S. Beals. Professor Beals, his family, and the first female students lived in "the mansion," as it came to be known. The girls were often crammed twelve to a room. By 1871, male and female dormitories had been completed, and the school had received a state charter. The state of Mississippi provided minimal funding throughout the 1880s, but this ended with the restrictive constitution of 1890.

Masonry courses were taught at the high-school-level institution, and the seven buildings that joined the Boddie Mansion were built largely with student labor. In 1897, a college-level department was begun, and its first graduates received their diplomas in 1901. In 1916, the school was officially named Tougaloo College. It struggled through decades of segregation and funding crises, and the mansion struggled along with it. Early in the century, a sleeping porch was added across the second-floor facade; the interior spaces were subdivided for offices and classrooms. Partial renovations kept the old house from completely collapsing. It witnessed some of the most significant civil rights demonstrations held in Mississippi, and was visited by Dr. Martin Luther King, Jr., Attorney General Robert Kennedy, Medgar Evers, Joan Baez, and myriad other leaders of the movement.

By the 1990s, the mansion was in hazardous shape. A multimillion dollar renovation project began in 2002 and continues, assuring John Williams Boddie's ill-fated home a future in this haven of educational opportunity.

AMMADELLE

Most of Oxford and Lafayette County's antebellum mansions are a stark interpretation of Greek Revival, frame structures with simple paired box columns and tall, narrow porticoes. Their builder, more often than not, was William Turner, a talented but likely self-taught carpenter with little or no formal architectural training. He was responsible for a number of these strikingly similar houses, all elegant but with a notable lack of exterior decoration. They are memorable in their austerity.

William Turner oversaw the work on one exceptional project, dramatically different from his usual creations, that was actually designed by one of America's most famous architects. Ammadelle is an elaborate confection of gables and window hoods and shaped bricks, an Italianate landmark in a region known for Greek Revival simplicity. Its architect was Calvert Vaux, one of the most celebrated house and landscape designers of his day. While little is known about William Turner other than the houses he left behind, Vaux's career is extensively documented. He

was born in England in 1822, migrated to America after an aborted apprenticeship, and went to work with Andrew Jackson Downing, the popularizer of Romantic architecture in mid-nineteenth-century America. After Downing's death in a Hudson River steamboat explosion, Vaux claimed his mantle and published his own house-pattern book, the 1857 *Villas and Cottages*. He then teamed up with landscape architect Frederick Law Olmsted to craft the winning design of a "greensward" for Manhattan, which would

evolve into Central Park. Vaux supplied the drawings and laid out the park, but left the implementation to Olmsted. That left him free to take building commissions, such as the one proposed by Thomas Pegues of Oxford, Mississippi.

How Pegues, a planter and railroad investor who had gone from living in a log cabin at Woodson's Ridge to owning four thousand acres and 150 slaves, came to be familiar with Calvert Vaux's work is unknown. Pegues was a close friend of University of Mississippi chancellor Frederick A. P. Barnard, a native New Yorker, and Barnard may have arranged an introduction. Pegues wanted a house in Oxford, close to the square, and in preparation for that eventuality he planted a line of oak trees going from the square and up North Street (now North Lamar Avenue), all the way to his one-hundred-acre lot. Intrigued by the drawings in Vaux's book, he travelled to New York to discuss Design #27 and view some of the architect's projects in the Hudson River valley. Design #27 had recently been erected in Middletown, Connecticut;

Ammadelle features gracefully arched windows throughout.

{ 93 }

after seeing that house, Pegues knew he had found the plan he wanted. It was rumored to cost almost fifteen thousand dollars, a phenomenal amount for 1850s Lafayette County.

Calvert Vaux drew up sixteen pages of detailed drawings, signing each in the lower right-hand corner. He may or may not have viewed the actual site for the house; as was his tendency, once his drawings were complete, he left the actual building details to others, in this case William Turner. Turner had the house partially completed when the Civil War started. It is by far the most unusual in Oxford, a town noted for its Greek Revival preference. Set far back from North Lamar Avenue in a grove of trees and boxwoods, it is a two-story red brick Italianate design with an abundance of details. Arched windows are topped with stone balustrades and hoods. The roof gables meet at eccentric angles. The front facade is dominated by a flat-roofed one-story balustraded porch. Bricks burned on the grounds were curved and molded to create window hoods and bay windows. Inside, a broad foyer opens into double parlors separated by sliding doors. A library and a conservatory are heated by hot water pipes. Unusual features include built-in closets, almost unheard of in the antebellum era, two bathrooms with running water, and an attached kitchen dominated by an enormous fireplace.

Thomas Pegues named the house Edgecomb, moved his family in, and made do with the incom-

plete structure as war swept in and around Oxford. After Federal troops set fire to the square in August 1864, they headed up North Street. Pegues had helped to equip and outfit Confederate troops, and this may have been known to General A. J. Smith, who turned his troops loose on the undefended town. Soldiers burst into Edgecomb with torches blazing. Flames had just been laid upstairs when the sound of approaching Confederate soldiers sent the Federals

scurrying. The family beat out the flames before they spread. The charred floorboards can still be seen on the second level.

The house was finally finished after the war. It was bought by Charles Roberts and later sold to his business partner, banker Bem Price. Price was reported to be the wealthiest man in early 1900s Oxford, and he combined the names of his sister, Amma, and his wife, Della, to create a new house name, Ammadelle. His

Left: Calvert Vaux's design was nearly destroyed by Union marauders.
Right: Ammadelle is the most elaborately decorated Italianate mansion extant in Mississippi.

widow later left the house to her niece, who in turn sold it to David Neilson. Neilson modernized the massive house and added the porches on the north side, along with window hoods and bracketing. Over the course of the twentieth century, further improvements were made by several families, but Calvert Vaux's original design has remained evident. Some William Faulkner scholars have surmised that Thomas Pegues and Calvert Vaux may have been the inspiration for Thomas Sutpen and his French architect in *Absalom, Absalom!*

Ammadelle was bought by the Tatum family several decades ago, and they have faithfully maintained the house and grounds as envisioned by Pegues and Vaux.

The rounded arches of Ammadelle are a characteristic feature of the Italianate style.

MOUNT HOLLY

The Yazoo-Mississippi Delta, that crescent of land stretching from Memphis to Vicksburg and east from the Mississippi River to the loess bluffs, would depend on agricultural pursuits long after the fields around such early Cotton Kingdom towns as Natchez, Columbus, and Holly Springs were exhausted. But for all its association with cotton, the Delta was a latecomer to development, almost totally missing the antebellum era with respect to its architecture and cultural history. The few exceptions are found around Lake Washington and near Greenville, an area which attracted wealthy settlers from Kentucky and South Carolina in the decades preceding the Civil War. These intrepid pioneers faced obstacles far greater than their counterparts farther south on the river or inland in Mississippi. Not only was their chosen land saturated with bears and alligators and malignant mosquitoes, but in any given spring season the Mississippi River might choose to inundate and obliterate all that they had worked to build. Hundreds of acres sloughed off into the river's currents on a regular basis, and more than one grand house, built by

planters who thought they could tame the Father of Waters, met the same fate.

Henry Johnson was one of the earliest settlers in the Lake Washington area, joining other wealthy Kentuckians in search of the incredibly rich Delta land along the river. In 1833, he bought several thousand acres from John Miller and set his one hundred slaves to work clearing stumps and planting the first cotton. Johnson maintained homes in Kentucky and New Orleans as well as in Washington County. His daughter, Margaret, married into an equally prominent Kentucky family. Her husband, James Erwin, was first married to the daughter of Senator Henry Clay. Margaret Johnson Erwin raised the children of that union as well as two that she bore Erwin.

James Erwin died in 1851, leaving Margaret a considerable fortune to blend with her own. Rather than retreating to the relative safety and civilization of her Kentucky family, she chose to build a house near her father's place on Lake Washington. He wasn't a particularly benevolent parent, charging Margaret the then-

astronomical sum of one hundred thousand dollars for seventeen hundred acres of his plantation. The site overlooks the northeastern corner of the lake, an oxbow formed by the shifting of the Mississippi River's currents.

Over the next several years, Margaret remarried, gave birth to one more son, and planned her house. Mount Holly was most likely under construction by 1855. It bears a striking resemblance to a Calvert Vaux design featured in a *Harper's Weekly* drawing of that same year. The actual architect and builder of the house are unknown; if they did emulate the Vaux drawing, their lack of sophistication may be seen in some of the details and proportions omitted from what remains a strikingly beautiful house. It is reputedly very similar to Aldemar, a huge house that was being built by Margaret Erwin's cousin, Junius Ward, at the same time. Ward was one of those intrepid Deltonians who chose to ignore nature's dominance; his mansion crumbled into the river before completion.

Mount Holly is a two-story Italianate structure of orange brick, encompassing fourteen thousand square

feet of space in thirty rooms. The primary entrance faces west, looking out over Lake Washington, and features a projecting gabled center section with a Palladian arch, an iron balcony fronting two paired arched windows, and a circular ornament below the bracketed eaves. A single-story porch with rounded arches stretches across the north side. Bay windows and a multiarched porch, topped with a balustaded roof railing, add to the Italianate design of the house. Corbeled chimneys are dotted across the low slanted roof.

On the interior, Mount Holly incorporates the typically irregular floor plan of Italianate houses. Its entrance hallway includes statuary niches and is flanked by drawing rooms, dining rooms, a library, conservatory, and a separate stair hall. Stretching away from the main house in an ell-wing are the kitchen and a smokehouse attached by a porch, along with privies. On the second level, numerous bedrooms and a ballroom have been altered over the years to provide bathrooms and closet space.

It took four years to complete Mount Holly, and the family moved there in 1859. An avenue of live oaks was planted on the carriage path leading to the house, and for several years it was the social center of Washington County. War reached the area in 1863, but the skirmishes and destruction that struck other parts of the county spared Margaret Erwin's family and home. She died in the summer of 1863, leaving instructions in her will to sell the house and divide the proceeds equally among James Erwin's children and her own three. The will was not honored, and the house remained in the possession of her widower, Charles Dudley, and his son, Charles Dudley, Jr. Charles, Jr., died there in 1893, and the house passed through a series of owners, including Sharkey County sheriff Huger Lee Foote, the inspiration for grandson Shelby Foote's main character in his novel *Tournament*.

The Lee, Griffin, and Cox families owned and preserved Mount Holly throughout much of the twentieth century. It survived the record-breaking flood of 1927 and temporarily served as the region's relief headquarters. The Coxes offered the house to the state for use as an interpretive park in 1972. Instead of seizing this opportunity to preserve and interpret one of the state's most unique antebellum homes, money was used to build a replica of a Greek Revival house near Greenwood. Mount Holly has struggled for survival ever since, briefly serving as a bed-and-breakfast inn. It is now used only for private functions and awaits restoration.

Mount Holly is one of the few surviving antebellum houses on Lake Washington.

Gothic Revival

In the 1840s, a style of domestic architecture drastically different from the prevailing Greek Revival began to appear in the northeastern United States. The steep roofs, carved vergeboards, and pointed arches of Gothic Revival were promoted by Alexander Jackson Davis in his 1837 pattern book, *Rural Residences*, and by Andrew Jackson Downing in his 1842 *Cottage Residences* and 1850 *Architecture of Country Houses*. These two architects were expanding on a trend begun almost a century before in England, when Horace Walpole renovated his country house with battlements and pointed-arch windows. The result was reminiscent of the ancient castles and cathedrals of Britain and came to be known as Gothic Revival. It enjoyed a degree of popularity in England before appearing in America, where Davis and Downing became its chief proponents. They emphasized the beauty of rural life and the harmony between functional "cottages" and their natural surroundings.

Gothic Revival made very little impact on the Greek Revival–dominated tastes of antebellum Mississippians. As with Italianate styling, Gothic homes were

more difficult and more expensive to build and less easily mastered by untrained carpenters. Several landmark examples have survived, however, and their individual elements represent many of the eccentric characteristics of Gothic Revival.

The Manship House, near downtown Jackson, is an almost exact replication of "Design XXIV" from A. J. Downing's *Architecture of Country Houses*. It features the center cross-gable with elaborately carved bargeboards, carved finials, double lancet-arched windows, and clustered chimneys, all elements of Gothic Revival. It is now owned and preserved as a house museum by the Mississippi Department of Archives and History.

Holly Springs claims two of the most outstanding Gothic Revival houses in the state, both on the same

street. William Henry Coxe's 1858 Airliewood is a pink stucco, multigabled villa with numerous finials and parapets, set within estate-size grounds. Bay windows and drip molds above the windows mark its Gothic theme. A few hundred yards to the east is Cedarhurst, completed in 1857. Specially molded bricks are used here to create the window arches, and iron tracery lines the porch roof and the three front-facing gables. The porch of Airliewood has been extensively altered during the twentieth century, but Cedarhurst is unchanged from the days when writer Sherwood Bonner grew up there.

Despite the relative dearth of Gothic Revival homes in Mississippi, the style is represented by its incorporation into Greek Revival homes of the late 1850s. Walter Place, also in Holly Springs, has impressive three-story octagonal towers flanking its center classical facade. In Columbus, several houses of the Columbus Eclectic style have baskethandle arches and tracery reminiscent of the Gothic mode.

Intricate ironwork at Cedarhurst

MANSHIP HOUSE

—Jackson

The City of Jackson wears mourning to-day; the voice of the people is hushed; the grief of the people is deep; for C. H. Manship is no more. After a long life, spent honorably, bravely and happily, he has gone forth to even a 'Better Life' in a fairer land than this. It seems peculiarly fitting that a man such as he was, who had lived the life he had, even unto the end thereof, upheld by the respect of a City, cared for by a host of friends, and beloved by an unusually large and peculiarly affectionate circle of relatives, should have met the end as he did, quietly, peacefully, in the home which had been his pride through a long life.[35]

Kate Power wrote this memorial more than a century ago. In the decades since, Charles Manship's "country villa" has been swallowed up by urban progress and neighborhood change. He and his wife, Adaline, are buried just a few blocks south of the Manship House, in Jackson's Greenwood Cemetery. The curators at Manship's Gothic home still occasionally drape the house in mourning, recalling the sense of

loss which all of Jackson felt at the passing of this remarkable man. Artist, civic leader, fireman, and mayor of Jackson on its darkest day, he was a man whose spirit still seems to hover about the dim hallways of the Manship House. The black crape draped over the arched entryway and cascading off the door-

bell are reminders that some people leave a permanent impression on their creations.

Charles Henry Manship was apprenticed as a teenager in his native Maryland to a decorative painter and chairmaker. His talents in painting, woodgraining, and marbling brought him to Jackson in 1836. Mississippi and its capital city were booming, and that prosperity was reflected in the early mansions of North State Street and the emerging facades of the statehouse, Governor's Mansion and city hall. Homeowners and taxpayers wanted elegant homes and public buildings, and Manship's artistry found immediate demand. He quickly formed a partnership with James Waugh, and the two advertised their services in the March 3, 1836, *Mississippian*:

Waugh & Manship, have permanently located themselves in the town of Jackson, and offer their services in all the branches of the above business; and, with a practical knowledge and strict personal attention to business, hope to merit a share of public patronage.

Left: Carved woodwork and lancet windows are Gothic elements.
Right: The Manship House was home to Jackson's Civil War–era mayor.

Persons wanting painting done, of any description, will do well to call on the subscribers, on [the] Street one square north of the State-House.

Manship was scurrying all over the young city, juggling numerous jobs, including the decoration of the statehouse. He worked there under the direction of its contractor, David Daley, whose daughter, Adaline, would become Mrs. Manship. The newlyweds bought a small house on President Street and began their family. In 1839, Manship partnered with James Ross and painted the Jackson City Theatre; that partnership would continue until Ross's death in 1843. From that point on, Manship apparently worked alone out of his shop on Pascagoula Street, where he also sold wallpapers, paint, and varnish.

Manship devoted his time to his adopted community, serving as city clerk in 1848, chairman of the Lunatic Asylum Building Commission in 1850, and as the primary contractor in repairing and painting the Governor's Mansion in the mid-1850s. Business was good. Manship's family was expanding as quickly as his reputation, and by the late 1850s, they had outgrown their President Street home. Seven children, all under the age of fifteen, prompted the building of a substantial house. Manship chose a lot on the northern edge of Jackson and likely utilized "Design XXIV" from Andrew Jackson Downing's 1850 *Architecture of Country Houses.* Downing called it "A Cottage-Villa in

the Rural Gothic Style" and designed the original for William Rotch of New Bedford, Massachusetts. The text describes it in detail: "The body of the house is nearly square, and the elevation is a successful illustration of the manner in which a form usually uninteresting, can be so treated as to be highly picturesque. There is, indeed, a combination of the aspiring lines of the roof with the horizontal lines of the veranda, which expresses picturesqueness and domesticity very successfully."[36]

Manship altered Downing's plan to fit his own needs and the demands of the steamy southern climate. It was reduced from a two-story to a one-story house with a longer central hall; the windows were extended to stretch from floor to ceiling. A fifty-foot porch faces the west, with a dominating center gabled bay. A sharply pointed triangular pediment is accentuated by a band of dentil molding at its base and intricately carved bargeboards. A carved finial pendant hangs from the apex; rising from the arch is another finely carved finial. Centered in the pediment is a characteristic ornament of Gothic Revival, a double lancet-arch window with a cutout quatrefoil. The long veranda is outlined in grapevine-inspired wrought iron, as is the porch on the south elevation. Three clustered chimneys accentuate the roofline.

Inside, Manship spent ten years decorating the halls and rooms. The broad central hallway, with sixteen-foot ceilings, is lined with wallpaper that incorporates

vertical frames. The pine and cypress doors are grained to imitate mahogany. The dining room appears to be wood-paneled, but closer inspection reveals its surface to be wallpapering over rough plaster, painted to resemble wood. Altogether, the house consists of a formal parlor, three bedrooms, a sitting room, bathing room, and dining room.

Over a twenty-six-year span, the Manships had fifteen children, ten of whom survived beyond infancy. Manship was as creative with names as he was with paint, dubbing two of his daughters Louisiana and Vicksburg. By the time of the Civil War, his brood was tumbling about a lot that included the main house, a cistern, a separate kitchen, and probably a barn and slave quarters. Records indicate that the Manship family owned at least one slave.

Manship was elected mayor of Jackson in 1862, an ill-timed honor that he may have come to regret. He watched his town burn as Union troops swept in and out in 1863, and in July of that year he surrendered the city to General Sherman. The war crept right into the Gothic mansion on West Street. Family tales relate how Addie, one of the Manship daughters, watched Federal soldiers overturn a barrel of molasses in the living room, smash the china, and set fire to the floors. Her cries of distress convinced them to extinguish the blaze before it consumed the house. Her mother, hoping for a degree of immunity from the troops because of her New England roots, nevertheless leaned toward

Curators drape the Manship House in Victoria-era mourning each fall.

caution. She tied the family silver to her waist and lowered it beneath her hoop skirts. Her servants were instructed to pull the wheels from the family carriage and hide them in a pond lest the carriage be taken by troops. It is unclear how successful her efforts were, but the house at least was spared, a rare feat in the desolation of "Chimneyville."

Reconstruction and the late 1800s brought happier times to the Manship House, which was rapidly becoming an urban home as Jackson grew north around it. Manship served as the captain of the local volunteer fire department, as postmaster, and as a trustee for the Blind Institute. Jefferson Davis visited the house and left an engraved portrait of himself. Children grew up, grandchildren came along, and in 1888 the entire clan gathered for Charles and Adaline's golden wedding anniversary. It was, of course, noted in the *New Mississippian* on December 12, 1888:

Mr. and Mrs. C. H. Manship to-day, at their lovely home, celebrate the fiftieth anniversary of their mar-

riage. This pleasant event which is vouchsafed to but few—very few, is also made the occasion of a happy family re-union, the first enjoyed by them in years. Mr. and Mrs. Manship were married just a half century ago, in this city, and their wedded union has been blessed with fifteen children, ten of whom still survive, all grown to the estate of man and womanhood; and it is a family of children, too, upon whom any parent might well look with pride and affection. Mr. Manship has long since passed the allotted years of three-score and ten, and now enjoys the distinction of being Jackson's oldest resident.[37]

Charles Henry Manship lived another seven years on West Street, dying at age eighty-three in 1895. Adaline lived on there until her own death in 1903. The house passed through several generations of the Manship family, which grew to include Paul Manship, sculptor of the Prometheus statue in Rockefeller Center; Mississippi lieutenant governor Luther Manship; and juvenile court judge Luther Manship, Jr. In its

later years, the house was only sporadically occupied. It served as the site for the last Confederate veterans' reunion in Mississippi in 1937.

In 1975, the house was deeded to the Mississippi Department of Archives and History. Restoration began in 1978. Archeological work located the site of the original detached kitchen north of the main house. An attached 1910 kitchen was removed, revealing the original drab olive-and-cream paint scheme on the house's exterior. A few sections of the original cast iron had to be replaced, as did the rooftop finial. The steps were reconstructed, layers of wallpaper stripped off, and the original patterns reproduced from fragments found beneath door frames and in closets. Furnishings, some original to the house, reflect the family's life at the time of the 1888 anniversary celebration. Throughout the year, occasions such as Halloween, Thanksgiving, and Christmas are observed in authentic Victorian fashion, and thousands of Mississippi schoolchildren are introduced to a remarkable man and his enduring legacy on West Street.

CEDARHURST

In the first twenty-five years of its existence, Holly Springs enjoyed several periods of remarkable prosperity, none more exuberant than the late 1850s. During that decade, the success of the community's leaders was reflected in the Greek Revival mansions that lined Salem Street and dotted the neighborhoods surrounding the square. Montrose, Athenia, Wakefield, and countless others, with their fanlighted pediments and Corinthian columns, stand as perfect examples of Mississippi's architectural excellence in that era.

Around the country, Gothic Revival styling was rivaling, if not replacing, the classic formalism of the Greek Revival, but it found expression in very few Mississippi towns. Holly Springs was an exception. Two of Marshall County's most prosperous citizens did build memorable Gothic homes there, both of which are fortunately extant and standing within a block of each other. Airliewood was the home of William Henry Coxe. Across Salem Street and just east of that house was the home of Dr. Charles Bonner and his daughter, Katherine Sherwood Bonner, a gifted

writer who would shake the foundations of respectable Victorian womanhood. Cedarhurst, as the Bonner house came to be known, has been owned by only two families in the entire century and a half of its history.

Charles Bonner was the Pennsylvania-born son of Irish immigrants. Having completed his medical training, he set out for the booming frontier town of Huntsville, Alabama, and soon afterwards migrated on to Marshall County, Mississippi. One of the county's first physicians, Dr. Willis Lea, took Bonner in as a partner. He also introduced the young doctor to Mary Wilson at the Lea mansion, Wildwood. Dr. Bonner married Mary and merged her inheritance of land and money with his own career as a planter/physician. Four children were born to the couple, and the social standards of the day dictated that they be raised in a fine house. Dr. Bonner bought a lot, reputedly at the highest elevation in Marshall County, in order to move his wife and children into Holly Springs. He contracted with architect Thomas Kelah Wharton to fashion an unusual Gothic house, which was completed in

Cedarhurst features a variety of window and door shapes.

1857. It would be the repository of the earliest memories of young Katherine, known to her friends and family as Kate, but destined to be remembered in the world of letters as the writer Sherwood Bonner.

The house that Kate Bonner grew up in was essentially the structure that stands today. In true Gothic fashion, it is a multigabled brick house with dramatic pointed arches derived from careful brick placement around the windows and doors. Elaborately carved bargeboards hang beneath the eaves. Finials and pendants outline the roof. Ironwork from the Jones McElwain Foundry adds elaborate detailing; paired octagonal chimneys dominate the roofline. University of Mississippi professor Alexander Bondurant described the Bonner House around 1900:

> It is a commodious brick mansion, built in Gothic style, with a wide portico in front, and ample windows opening to the floor. The house stands well back from the street, surrounded by a spacious lawn. One enters a wide hall, and on the left is seen the library, where in winter a wood fire is kept burning. The room is a very charming one, and afforded a most appropriate setting for the writer at her desk.[38]

"[T]he writer at her desk" whom Bondurant was describing was Kate Bonner, eldest child of Charles and Mary Bonner. She thrived in the unusual house and its outbuildings throughout her youth, soaking

Left: The window arches of Cedarhurst are formed by specially shaped bricks.
Right: Only two families have owned Cedarhurst in its century-and-a-half of existence.

up stories told by the family slaves in the detached kitchen. She would later describe that room as "the pleasantest place in the world . . . with its roomy fireplace, where the backlog glowed and the black kettle swung."[39] She absorbed the atmosphere of her secure antebellum world and demonstrated her writing talent with her first nationally published story at age fifteen.

The Bonner family's idyllic life on Salem Street was interrupted by war just a few years after they moved to town. In 1862, Union troops were threatening to sweep into north Mississippi. Dr. Bonner received an executive order from Governor J. J. Pettus to immediately establish a hospital in Holly Springs. He chose one of the most commodious buildings in town, Holly Springs Female Institute, where Kate happened to be enrolled. Classes were cancelled in March 1862, and the first casualties from Shiloh rolled in just a few weeks later.

Life in Holly Springs and at the Bonner House would never be the same. There was a lull during the summer and early fall of 1862, when the Bonners and their neighbors enjoyed the excitement of hosting Confederate general Sterling Price and his troops. Parties and balls were the order of the day. But all that changed as Grant moved into north Mississippi and Price slipped south with his command. Kate Bonner, thirteen, watched from her home:

> *It was a sad day when the army left, for we bade friends good-bye to prepare for foes. Boxes of silver were buried at night under flowerbeds or ash heaps; gold pieces were secured in leather belts; doors were locked and windows barred. Then we waited until one bright morning in December, when frightened Negroes came flying in from the country round with the dread news, "The Yankees are coming!"* [40]

War would rage in and out of Holly Springs for the next three years, often invading the Bonner house itself as Dr. Bonner moved recuperating soldiers in and tents were pitched on the lawn. When Union forces occupied Holly Springs, an American flag was draped from the second-floor balcony of the house; Kate and her siblings staged a silent revolt by going out of their

Sherwood Bonner described the devastation of war and yellow fever as she witnessed them from Cedarhurst.

way to avoid walking beneath it. With Holly Springs Female Institute permanently closed, Kate was sent away to boarding school in Montgomery, Alabama. She returned in the summer of 1863 to find the Bonner house standing intact and largely unmolested, but Holly Springs as a whole devastated. "I should never have recognized in the dreary village the once prosperous, comfortable little town. Weeds grew rank everywhere, and desolation hung over all things like a funeral pall."[41]

The Bonners made do. Mrs. Bonner, as the war wore on, grew quite adept at hiding family goods and livestock from foraging soldiers. At one point, she herded their last three chickens into the attic and shooed two pigs into the cellar; all were discovered and confiscated. The war drew to its inevitable conclusion, but the finality of defeat was still a shock to Kate. She was walking toward town from the Bonner house when an elderly neighbor ran up to her. "In the white wild face that he turned toward us there was such an agony as I have never seen . . . He looked at us a moment in silence, then in a hollow, harsh voice struck us with the words, 'General Lee has surrendered!' and passed on into the falling darkness."[42]

Kate's mother lived only a few months after the war's end. Dr. Bonner sent for his maiden sister, "Aunt Martha," to look after his children. He could then take on a leading role in making peace with the occupying forces of Reconstruction. Neighbors were scandalized

when he invited Union officers to church; they were apoplectic when he rented the top floor of the Bonner house to General Ord and his staff. For another ten years, he would hold the homeplace together, through the travails of Reconstruction.

Kate's marriage to Edward McDowell and the birth of their daughter, Lilian, brought a short-lived levity to the Bonner house. Dr. Bonner had to endure the local

gossip when Kate left her husband and child to live in Boston, fulfilling her literary aspirations as Henry Wadsworth Longfellow's protégé and secretary. Her writing career was on the upswing when she rushed home to care for her father and brother, both stricken with yellow fever in the 1878 epidemic. Kate came home to a "plague-stricken place" where "[t]runks were packed hastily . . . houses were left unlocked unguarded.

Dr. Bonner scandalized Holly Springs by renting his upstairs rooms to Union officers.

In the streets, carriages, buggies, wagons, anything on wheels, hurried along, loaded down with those who, from lack of money or any other reason, could not get away by rail. Dearest friends passed each other with only a hand-grip . . . fearing never to meet again."[43]

Kate squeezed Lilian and Aunt Martha onto the last train out of the stricken town, then telegraphed Longfellow: "Help for God's sake. Send money. Father and brother down yellow fever. Alone to nurse."[44] Her father and brother would live only a few days, dying within hours of each other in the solitude of the Bonner house. As with the hundreds of other yellow fever victims, their bodies were hurriedly dispatched to the cemetery. Kate closed up the house and somehow managed to slip through the quarantine, returning to her friends in Boston. After the first life-saving frost halted the spread of yellow fever, she returned home to Holly Springs, writing back to a concerned Longfellow: "I am at home again, if this great desolate house can be called home."[45]

Kate's days of freedom in Boston were over. She struggled through the scandal of a divorce and searched for ways to maintain her home. Foreclosure was a constant threat, leading her to once again write her famous benefactor in Boston. "And you will help, will you not, to save my home to secure for myself a retreat for my ruined life where I may die with dignity."[46] Longfellow sent her a check for five hundred dollars shortly before his death in 1882. Devastated by that loss, Kate ignored the warning signs of her own illness. She was finally diagnosed with an aggressive breast cancer and frantically plunged into literary work that would support Lilian and Aunt Martha. Friends took dictation from the fading writer in her bedroom at the Bonner house. She died there, aged thirty-four, on July 22, 1888. Eulogies poured in from across the country, none more eloquent than that of her childhood friend Helen Craft Anderson: "To literature she was 'Sherwood Bonner,' the young author full of genius and promise; to society she was the beautiful, fascinating woman, always the central attraction in every room she entered; but to the companions of her youth she was only 'Kate,' the loyal, brave, trusted friend, whose untimely death has taken so much from life that it can never look the same again."[47]

Lilian McDowell and Aunt Martha stayed on at the Bonner house, desperately trying to preserve the aging structure. They took in boarders and struggled along until the house was put up for public auction on March 2, 1889. A mysterious friend of Kate's, Colton Greene of Memphis, rescued them by buying it and deeding it back to the family. He would eventually will his considerable estate to Lilian. After Aunt Martha's death, Lilian sold the house to William Alexander Belk, a distinguished educator, jurist, and state senator. It has passed through three subsequent generations of the Belk family, always maintained and preserved, and remains one of the state's preeminent examples of Gothic Revival architecture.

AIRLIEWOOD

In the mid-1800s, Andrew Jackson Downing, a New York architect, popularized a style of domestic architecture that contrasted dramatically with the prevailing Greek Revival mode of columns and classical forms. His Gothic Revival homes were widely publicized as "villas," appropriate for the gentleman farmer and well-to-do suburbanite. The styles were elaborate and multifaceted, with carved brackets and towers and deeply pointed arched windows and doors. They were fairly common throughout the Northeast but rare in the South, where the practicality of broad verandas and high ceilings kept Greek Revival dominant long after its day had passed elsewhere.

William Henry Coxe commissioned Thomas Kelah Wharton and the German Rittlemeyer brothers to build one of Downing's designs on a fifteen-acre estate in Holly Springs, Mississippi. Coxe had moved to Mississippi from Georgia, along with four of his brothers, to take over land bought on speculation by their father. They built one of the great antebellum plantation houses of Marshall County—Galena, a sprawling

one-story Greek Revival house southwest of Holly Springs. William Henry decided at some point to move his wife, Amelia, and daughter, Lida Victoria, into town, possibly to escape the antics of his brothers, who were known as some of Marshall County's more uninhibited citizens.

As it originally existed, Airliewood was a two-story brick structure, covered with stucco that was scored to resemble stone. Sharply arched windows with hoods and tall, lancet-shaped doors contributed to the vertical effect. The decorated bargeboards and spires lent decoration to the overall effect. Local historian John Mickle described it in 1930:

> Since it was built about 1858, the Will Henry Cox[e] place on Salem Avenue has been one of the show places of Holly Springs . . . The house is said to have cost $[6]0,000, and building could be done much cheaper then than now, with the best materials plentiful and cheap. It is designed in the perpendicular gothic style, which was observed in all particulars.

The gates and fence at Airliewood were used for target practice by Union soldiers.

The halls above and below are sixteen feet wide and run the length of the house. There are four rooms on each floor; large and high pitched with a wing at the back in which are located a beautiful sitting room, with pantries and kitchen. The two parlors on the west side are connected by an archway, the rear and smaller room having a bay window. One or two were added to the rear of the house by later owners. The windows and veranda are in keeping with the gothic style, and add much to the beauty of the house. As far as conveniences went, the house was well provided for that time. It was piped for gas throughout and the chandeliers were artistic in hammered iron. The bathroom with running water was so far as known the first installed in Holly Springs. Water for it was pumped by hand. A system of call bells from all rooms was also arranged. The grounds which Mr. Cox[e] bought in 1858 contained about fifteen acres, the front of it covered with large forest trees, many of which have yielded to time and the elements, but enough are left to give beauty to the place.[48]

The interior of Airliewood features high ceilings, an impressive stair, marble mantels, silver doorknobs, and a bathtub built from a solid square of lead. Outbuildings, including a stable, kitchen, and servants' quarters, were designed to match the house. Separating the grounds from busy Salem Street is an impressive fence, possibly cast at the local Jones McElwain Foundry,

Airliewood sheltered General and Mrs. Grant during occupation of Holly Springs.

with a gate fashioned by Wood & Perrot of Boston to match one at the United States Military Academy. Altogether, the house, grounds, and fence set Mr. Coxe back over sixty thousand dollars, an enormous sum in antebellum Mississippi.

The house was completed in 1858, too late for Amelia Coxe, who had died in 1857. Airliewood would play a central role in Holly Springs's involvement in the Civil War and its aftermath, although its owner was derided for his failure to partipate in military service. Mildred Strickland wrote indignantly to her husband, a Confederate officer, that "Jim House and Will H. Coxe go to dancing school,"[49] instead of leaving for the war as most of the town's men had done. After General Earl Van Dorn's dawn raid, General Ulysses Grant moved his headquarters and his family from Walter Place to the Coxe house, reputedly at the personal invitation of Mr. Coxe. Mrs. Grant fondly remembered her time there:

General Grant . . . retired to Holly Springs as he would be better situated for observing the field of action. At the request of Colonel [William H.] Coxe of this place, General Grant occupied his residence, a beautiful Italian villa. While here I frequently saw the young ladies of the Walker [sic] house. On some feast day—Christmas, I think—they sent me a fine turkey and some other poultry, which I was loath to accept, knowing how very valuable they must be,

and I wished I could return the compliment with some delicacies from the North, but our mess was always indifferent at best. All the nice things I had brought with me were long since gone.[50]

When Grant made plans to evacuate Holly Springs, Mrs. Grant rather reluctantly packed up her things and those of her son. Young Jesse's silver cup was missing, and William Henry Coxe attempted to smooth over the situation.

Colonel Coxe . . . stepped back to his dining room, and returned with a beautiful, slender-stemmed wineglass, saying, 'Will this answer, Mrs. Grant?' To my demur, not wishing to break his set of glass, he replied, 'Ah, no! Keep it as a souvenir of the house. I only wish I could add to it a bottle of rich, old wine, but mine is all gone.' And that slender, little pink glass was the only souvenir I ever brought from the South.[51]

Lida Victoria Coxe didn't always view the relationship as rosily as Mrs. Grant, who thought she was being gracious by inviting Lida to dine with her at Christmas. Holly Springs historian Olga Reed Pruitt noted that, for Lida, the "irony of being invited to dine in her own home goes without saying."[52] She also recounts a family tale of Lida coming in the front door and being surprised to see a Federal soldier lugging a bedspread down the stairs. He sheepishly admitted

that he was going to send it home to his mother. Other soldiers used the iron spikes on the fence for target practice. John Mickle recounted their deeds: "The panels of the fence carried spear heads which were broken off during the war of the sixties. Someone from Holly Springs while in Ohio a few years ago met an elderly man who said that he and another young Federal soldier in a spirit of boyish wantonness had knocked them off, and he was sorry to have marred the beauty of the fence."[53]

William Henry Coxe survived the war by staying home and perfecting his dance steps, only to die while drunkenly urging his horse up the steps of Airliewood. Colonel Dixon Comfort Topp, a Grenada County planter who had mysteriously survived the war with his fortune intact, bought Airliewood. Ten years later, with tensions between occupying Federal troops and Mississippians reaching crisis levels, Colonel Topp had run through his money and was renting rooms at Airliewood to the local Federal commander and his wife. Holly Springs was scandalized and Colonel Topp

ostracized. It would take the intervention of Mrs. Kate Freeman, the acknowledged arbiter of all things socially acceptable in the town, to restore order. She personally paved the way for interaction between townspeople and the Federal occupiers, allowing Holly Springs to avoid the riots which engulfed several Mississippi cities in those last days of Reconstruction.

Airliewood passed through several families over its next half-century. One of Mississippi's first female physicians, Dr. Fannie Elliott, along with her husband, bought the house and converted it into a hospital. George Stephenson was born there and recalled summer visits to the "sanitarium":

Next door to our house on the east was a large place that once was Grant's headquarters. I was born there, not because it had been built by a distant relative of mine, but because it was owned by Dr. and Mrs. Elliott (she was also a doctor) who ran it as a small hospital. We used to go over to handle the silver door knobs, pay our respects to the real skeleton in the

closet, and find out how the swarm of bees in an upstairs bedroom were getting along by listening to their thick hum through the wall. Dr. Elliott died, his wife went to Serbia after the war on a medical team, and Mr. Thompson bought the house.[54]

The Thompson family kept Shetland ponies, pigs, and cows on the large lot.

At some point, the original porch was torn off and a more battlement-like addition made. As regard for the Gothic style reached its lowest point, the old mansion was sold at a trustees' auction by the Bank of Holly Springs in 1929. Fortunately, it was bought by Mayor Charles Dean, a man who valued and preserved all facets of Holly Springs history. After his death, his widow had a whimsical, lancet-shaped swimming pool dug on the east lawn. The Dean family owned Airliewood until 1997, when it was saved from demolition by Mr. and Mrs. Lester G. Fant III. It is now undergoing renovation by the new owners, Mr. and Mrs. Joe Overstreet.

The dripmolds and battlements of Airliewood lend it a stark, brooding air.

Eclectic

A handful of antebellum houses in Mississippi defy ready classification into Federal, Greek Revival, Italianate, or Gothic Revival styles. All are products of the late 1850s building craze in which the state's forty-year reign as the Cotton Kingdom reached its apex architecturally. Greek Revival was still the prevailing mode of building in these late pre–Civil War years, but Italianate and Gothic Revival had gained a measure of legitimacy in areas of the South. Oriental and octagonal fashions were briefly popular but rarely translated into mansions. Waverley, Longwood, Walter Place, White Arches, and the Columbus Eclectic houses incorporated unique mixtures of some or all of the stylistic trends of the time, with a variety of interesting results.

Waverley is a stunning combination of a Greek Revival facade with an octagonal center cupola and an exceptional octagonal rotunda. Its H-shaped floor plan

is likely unique in American architecture. In nearby Columbus, White Arches is a riot of details, with columns that appear to be paneled but are actually octagonal posts. They are connected by rounded arches, which one would most often find on an Italianate house, and bracketed by porches with flattened arches of the Gothic mode. Rising above the porches is a multiwindowed octagonal tower.

Walter Place, in Holly Springs, is another unusual melding of styles. The formal proportions and columns of the central facade mark it as Greek Revival.

But flanking the center are two three-story crenellated towers with concrete ovals and battlements. Surprisingly, the overall effect is very graceful.

Far and away the most unusual house in Mississippi, eclectic or otherwise, is Longwood in Natchez. Dr. Haller Nutt commissioned Philadelphia architect Samuel Sloan to bring to life a design Sloan had playfully included in a pattern book. Sloan and Nutt's project was ill timed, however, and the Civil War left Longwood an eerie, echoing six-story shell, destined never to be finished. Its Italianate arches and Greek Revival columns compete with a massive Oriental dome, all wrapped up in a huge octagonal form. Had it been finished, Longwood would have been the true showplace of Natchez; in its present state, it is the most graphic reminder extant of the riches that built Mississippi's antebellum mansions and the war that sealed them forever in history.

WAVERLEY

—West Point

In the mid-1830s, Lucy Woodson Watkins Young, with her seven small children in tow, followed her husband, George Hampton Young, to the barely settled wilderness of Clay County, Mississippi. Colonel Young had purchased several thousand acres of prairie land following the Chickasaw Indian resettlement. The Youngs first built a house near West Point, but within a few years had moved out to "the upper place," close by the banks of the Tombigbee River. With their brood having now expanded to ten children, a spacious house was a necessity. Colonel Young put up a roomy two-story log structure, where Lucy had every intention of spending the rest of her life. But her husband had grander plans. He designed and began construction on the unique Greek Revival masterpiece that he would name Waverley.

Lucy Young cared little for the mansion rising in the woods. Her joy was the boxwood cuttings she had brought from her native Georgia, and she carefully set them out along the walkways leading to the house. She would not live to see the house completed around 1858, but her boxwoods would soar to fifteen feet and

live for almost a century and a half. For almost half of that period, it seemed that they would be the only element of the Young legacy to survive, as the house was closed and abandoned for fifty years. As the woods crept in around it and wildlife took over the parlors and bedrooms, it seemed doomed to oblivion. The story of its redemption by the Snow family is probably

the most remarkable restoration tale in Mississippi's architectural history.

George Hampton Young was a well-established lawyer and state legislator in Georgia when the Chickasaw lands came up for sale in 1832. He traveled with a manservant to Mississippi and bought several thousand acres for less than two dollars each. By 1836, he had brought his entire family and twenty-five slaves to West Point, then a tiny village a few miles west of the Tombigbee River. A decade later, he was ready to move out to the land he would name Waverley Plantation, in honor of Sir Walter Scott's Romantic novels. Financing the move was no problem. In addition to raising cotton on the rich prairie lands of Clay and Lowndes counties, he maintained cotton warehouses on the river and ran the local post office, a commissary, a steam mill, a cotton gin, a tanning yard, and his own ferryboat service. The 1850 census lists his property as including 117 slaves and two thousand acres of land, increasing by the time of the Civil War to 137 slaves and a personal estate of over three hundred thousand dollars.

Left: The Greek Revival office at Waverley probably predates the mansion.
Right: Waverley was abandoned for fifty years, all but disappearing in the Clay County forest.

No detailed description of the two-story log house survives. It was never adequate for a man like Colonel Young, whose vision for the ultimate Waverley was undoubtedly forming as soon as he moved in. He may have personally designed the mansion; Frazer Smith, in *White Pillars*, claims the existence of a diary (now lost, if it ever existed at all) which attributed the plan to St. Louis architect Charles Pond. Regardless of its origins, the result was a massive H-shaped Greek Revival house totally unlike anything else in the South. Fluted columns of cypress front a recessed gallery with an elaborate wrought-iron second-floor balcony. Marble steps and parapets, pilasters, and clapboard siding complement the facade. The striking front entrance is flanked by octagonal columns topped by Egyptian capitals. The front doorway is surrounded by sidelights and a transom of red Venetian glass with inlaid wooden lyres.

Inside, an overwhelming central hall soars upward fifty-five feet to an octagonal cupola with sixteen windows. Dangling from an ornate plaster ceiling medallion is a carved chandelier, originally gas-fired. Twin cantilevered stairs begin on opposite sides of the rear wall and turn repeatedly to reach the upper living level, then to an attic floor and finally to the cupola. Two sections of the stairway actually form bridges with no supporting framework. Lining the stair are 718 mahogany spindles. Flanking the main hall on the first level are a library, a dining room, the master bedroom, and a parlor with a built-in wedding alcove. Above are

four more bedrooms, each with the rare antebellum luxury of a closet.

The house's ventilation system is inspired. Each bedroom has a door opening onto the galleries; the cupola pulls steamy summer air up and out the clerestory windows, creating a permanent suction that cools the main room. The windows also serve to pour light down into that room, casting ever-varying shadows throughout the grand hall as the sun moves across the sky. In winter, a pine-fueled retort supplied gas through a series of pipes to the gasoliers located throughout the first floor.

As magnificent as the main house was, the outbuildings were numerous and impressive in their own right. The only extant example is the plantation office, a small brick temple-style building which likely predates the mansion. Over the years of abandonment, all the other structures were demolished or decayed completely. Lost were a barn, bathhouse, detached kitchen, cook's house, smokehouse, icehouse, privy, guesthouses, carriage house, and numerous slave cabins. Long since filled in was a swimming pool.

In 1858, the now-widowed Colonel Young moved his ten children into the mansion. Unlike many of his fellow plantation owners, he was an ardent secessionist and welcomed Mississippi's departure from the Union. Luckily for him, the war and Federal troops never threatened Waverley. Small skirmishes flared occasionally in proximity to the house, but no troops were known to have been on the plantation. Distant gunfire

led to a few scares and frantic loading of the family into surreys, always with a last-minute reprieve. The social whirl at Waverley went right on throughout the war. Even notorious Confederate spy Belle Edmonson was an extended houseguest. All six of the Young sons fought for the Confederacy; one was killed in action.

Colonel Young and his mansion survived the Civil War unscathed and barely blinked at Reconstruction. Many plantation owners struggled to hold on to their land and replace their lost slaves, but Young had enough sidelines to keep going. He actually prospered through the 1870s and left his children in excellent financial shape at the time of his death in 1880. All but two of those children married and moved out, leaving bachelors Valerius and William rambling about in the huge house by themselves. Nieces and nephews came and went and most of the former slaves stayed on as servants. When Valerius died in 1906, only William (or "Captain Billy," as he was affectionately known) was left. His gambling parties in the great hall were legendary, as was the annual "Independence Party" held each May for workers. Captain Billy's houseboy, Luke Richardson, had grown up at Waverley; when he married, he and his wife moved into the plantation office next to the main house.

Captain Billy died in 1913. His surviving sisters and their offspring had no interest in moving back out to Waverley, so the house was simply left alone, fully furnished and intact. For fifty long years, it was abandoned and ignored. One by one, the outbuildings were

The twin stairways of Waverley twist and curve from the main floor to the cupola.

taken over by tenant farmers and gradually fell apart or were demolished. Vines and bushes crept into the mansion, and the untended lawn grew wild, shielding the house from the road. Waverley was hardly forgotten; for generations, it was the favored gathering place for high school and college students. They partied there and left a thousand names scrawled on the plaster walls. By some unwritten code of honor, almost no structural damage was ever done to the old house other than that graffiti. The common assumption was that Waverley was irretrievable and doomed to a slow and ignominious implosion.

In 1962, antique dealers Robert and Donna Snow of Philadelphia, Mississippi, heard of the house from a salesman who had recently seen it. Intrigued, they drove to Clay County and scoured the woods until they found the site. Robert Snow describes their first impression:

We parked on the river road and walked through the dense growth toward some magnolia trees in the woods. We began to see fragments of the old gardens and a trail winding through the growth. As we came around a huge oak tree, we stopped dead in our tracks—absolutely breathless, mesmerized. There was the house rising up out of the jungle, four stories high with the dome set against the bluest sky. Vines clung to the house and swayed in the breeze. The porch floor had collapsed and the marble steps were scattered in the yard. We scarcely spoke. I climbed up on the porch and stuck my head through a broken red Venetian glass pane around the front door. The rotunda rose upward out of sight and balconies and stairs were everywhere! I whispered to Donna, "We've got to buy this place!" She looked at me like I was insane and said, "Robert Junior! You're crazy! This place is falling down." I took her hand and pulled her up to the door and told her to look. For a moment she said nothing at all. Then she whispered, "Oh . . . it is just beautiful."[55]

Despite the sad vista of the house, which had been neglected for a half-century, the Snows were hooked. They immediately made plans to buy it, ignoring the grime, massive dirt dauber nests, and bat colonies that filled the attic. The cupola had been taken over by bees, their undisturbed efforts having yielded a two-hundred-pound hive jammed with honey. The Snows moved in with their dubious maid and gardener. Robert's journal regarding that first night records the beginning of a thirty-year odyssey:

Donna and I, Bertha and Leonard all slept on the floor in the rotunda last night . . . In the dark we could hear owls hooting in the woods and wild animals stirring about the house. I slept little from the excitement. By dawn it was still as death. Gradually, daylight came into the cupola, and birds began to sing. As it became lighter, I watched as different elements of the architecture became visible. First, just the vastness of the space, then the stairways and the banisters and finally, slowly, the ornamental plaster on the ceiling four stories and 65 feet overhead. The birds and squirrels began to stir in the chandeliers and woodwork. It was truly magnificent.[56]

The Snows restored one room at a time, doing much of the work themselves with paintbrushes, toothpicks, and elbow grease. Each of the 718 stair spindles was carefully reworked, an eight-month task in itself. Their four children grew up in the vast rooms of Waverley and watched a miracle in progress. In 1975, Waverley received the coveted designation of National Historic Landmark. The Snows were awarded the first National Restoration Award, a well-deserved honor for years of dedication to one of Mississippi's irreplaceable treasures. Its doors are open to visitors almost every day, and over the years thousands have flocked down Waverley Mansion Road to marvel at Colonel Young's creation and hear the story of the devotion that saved it.

WHITE ARCHES

—Columbus

In the decade before the Civil War, three styles were predominant in American architecture. The Greek Revival craze, which had prevailed in the South for three decades, was waning. Italianate and Gothic houses were increasingly common but more expensive, complicated, and difficult to build without skilled craftsmen. A fourth style, the Octagonal, was so eccentric that it never truly caught on to any significant degree, but elements of it are seen in the detailing of many late-1850s homes. Longwood, in Natchez, is a rare example of a truly octagonal house; Waverley incorporates the octagon in its great rotunda. Holly Springs architect Spires Boling almost always found a way to work in eight-sided embellishments. Columbus features a number of houses with combinations of Greek Revival, Italianate, Gothic, and even Octagonal details, a hodgepodge that has come to be known as Columbus Eclectic.

White Arches is the ultimate example of Columbus Eclectic styling. The overwhelming abundance of arches, tower, doorways, and columns merge into a

visually stunning mixture. Its north facade is dominated by four thick pillars, each fashioned from octagonal posts. Rounded Italianate arches stretch between the pillars and are topped by an entablature. Rising above the entablature is a two-story octagonal tower with multiple full-length and narrow shuttered windows. Porches stretch along the front and the sides of White Arches, each outlined with patterned woodwork. Iron balconies wrap around the base of the tower and jut beneath the upstairs windows. A total of fifteen doors on two floors open to the out-

side; oddly enough, perhaps for security, most have no outside doorknobs.

Inside, a broad center hall divides double parlors on the right from a library, cross hall, and bedroom on the left. The main stair is mahogany, and a spiral stair rises from a smaller rear hallway. Upstairs are four additional bedrooms with closets, a rarity for the time. The tower houses a solarium accessible on the second level.

White Arches was built by Jeptha Vining Harris, a Mississippi state legislator and planter. Just four years after the completion of the house, Harris left to take a brigadier generalship in the Confederate army. In 1873, the house was sold to General Harris's brother-in-law, Dr. James Oliver Banks. Dr. Banks was a son-in-law of Colonel George Hampton Young of Waverley; these family connections linked two of the most unusual octagonally inspired houses in north Mississippi. White Arches passed down through several generations of the Banks family before being sold again. It has been meticulously restored and is a frequent inclusion on the Columbus Pilgrimage.

Above: White Arches has fifteen exterior doorways.
Following page: White Arches' design incorporates Greek Revival, Italianate, Gothic, and Octagonal elements.

WALTER PLACE

One of the most visually captivating houses in Mississippi sits a few blocks west of the Holly Springs square, separated by one mile and a broad artistic leap from the sedate Greek Revival mansions of Salem Street. Walter Place incorporates the columns and capitals of Greek Revival with surprising Gothic towers, battlements, and an eclectic mixture of details that set it apart from its contemporaneous neighbors. Its fortress-like demeanor is a reminder of the crises which the house has witnessed and endured, from war and occupation to an infectious scourge which nearly took Holly Springs off the map.

Harvey Washington Walter, described by an associate as "conspicuous in every public gathering . . . generous and magnanimous and . . . a Christian gentleman, by whose qualities all other men hereabouts were measured"[57] arrived in Marshall County in 1837. He was an Ohio teenager, thrust out on his own after his father's failure in the financial panic of that year. During the forty-one years he would live in Holly Springs, he spearheaded the birth of a railroad, helped plan a

courthouse, built a successful law practice, and raised ten children.

Walter first set himself up as a teacher in the tiny village of Salem, a few miles east of Holly Springs. Within the space of two years, he had passed the Mississippi bar and joined the throngs of lawyers clustering around the courthouse square in the state's most prosperous new county. His personality and strong work ethic brought financial success, and his reputation helped him win the hand of Fredonia Brown, daughter of a wealthy Oxford planter. Her dowry and

his rapidly accumulating fortune placed the Walter family in the upper echelons of Holly Springs society. The physical manifestation of that success, in mid-nineteenth-century Marshall County, nearly always involved the building of a fine house.

By the late 1850s, Walter was ready to add his unique twist to Mississippi architecture. He hired Spires Boling to be his architect and builder, as did most of Holly Springs's rich citizens. Boling's houses stand as masterpieces of Greek Revival beauty, but his most unique creations involved the use of the octagonal forms that were increasingly popular in that decade. He would slip in octagonal columns or an eight-sided dome in the design of otherwise purely Greek Revival structures. At Walter Place, whether through the urging of Harvey Walter or as a result of Boling's own imagination, the octagonal Gothic towers would be as dominant visually as the Greek Revival portico.

Walter Place today looks much as it did when Spires Boling completed it in 1860. The one exception is a small iron balcony which replaced the more elon-

Above: Tower at Walter Place
Previous page: Walter Place has endured wartime occupation, yellow fever deaths, and public auction.

gated original. Four white columns, topped with intricate Corinthian capitals, support a pedimented portico with an elliptical window. Five bays with stone-linteled windows are flanked by the multiwindowed towers.

If the facade ended with those five bays, it would be simply a reproduction of dozens of Greek Revival mansions from Natchez to Corinth. But Boling sandwiched the classical portico between two octagonal towers, each capped with stone battlements. Standing alone, they would evoke the image of English castles or Norman strongholds of the Middle Ages. Behind the towers, the roof is steeply pitched and gabled with elliptical fanlights in the gable ends.

The interior features a sweeping grand stair in the main hall, drawing and dining rooms, and multiple bedrooms. Bathrooms and studies are tucked into the old tower rooms. Ceilings on the first floor soar to sixteen feet and to fourteen feet on the upper level.

During the construction of his house, Walter was involved in numerous pursuits. Along with other Holly Springs businessmen, he had bankrolled the Mississippi Central Railroad's completion from Canton to Jackson, Tennessee. Walter personally turned the first spade of dirt in November 1858, and hammered in the final spike at Winona in January 1860. He ran unsuccessfully for governor on 1859's Whig ticket and lobbied long and hard as a Unionist opposed to secession. Just two months after moving

into Walter Place, he was down in Jackson, reluctantly voting with his fellow Marshall County representatives to pull Mississippi out of the Union. He undoubtedly knew this would lead to war, but he could not have

imagined that the conflict would soon land literally on his own doorstep.

The Battle of Shiloh and the Confederate defeat at Corinth in early 1862 gave Mississippians a wake-up call. The war that had seemed so remote when it raged in Virginia was now in their backyard. General Ulysses Grant fought through north Mississippi in November 1862, intent on capturing Vicksburg. He established his headquarters and supply station at Holly Springs, settled Mrs. Grant in at Walter Place, and pushed on to Oxford. Mrs. Grant was delighted with her accommodations. In her memoirs, she recalled her arrival in the occupied and surly little town:

From LaGrange, we went to Holly Springs . . . Jesse [her son] and Julia, my nurse and maid, a slave born and brought up at my old Missouri home [were also in Holly Springs] . . . Colonel Bowers had secured very nice quarters for us in a fine house belonging to Mr. Walker [sic], who, I think has formerly been a cabinet officer at Washington. It was occupied by the wife of a Confederate officer . . . She was a fine, noble woman, as so many of these Southern women were.[58]

Mrs. Grant, her son, and maidservant made themselves comfortable at Walter Place. Their "hostess" was Mary Govan, who, along with her daughter-in-law and two daughters, had been evicted from their own

The Greek Revival portico of Walter Place is balanced by Gothic towers.

home when it was commandeered for use as a hospital. Harvey Walter was away serving in the Confederate army; his family had fled to Huntsville. So the Grant entourage and the displaced Govan ladies settled in to make the best of an awkward situation. It was not without an element of tension. Before the arrival of Federal troops, the Govans had hastily buried their silver beneath the handmade bricks of the front sidewalk, and they would peep out of the tower windows worriedly as unsuspecting sentries marched back and forth, right over their horde. It was never discovered.

In the cold predawn hours of December 20, 1862, Confederate general Earl Van Dorn swept into Holly Springs with sixteen hundred men, routing the sleeping Federal troops and recapturing the town. He carved a path of destruction that equaled anything the Federals had wrought. Railroad cars were blown up, buildings torched, and munitions exploded. Mrs. Grant had left Walter Place only hours before in order to join her husband in Oxford. She later recalled hearing the news from Holly Springs:

The next morning, before we were fairly awake, a knock at our door announced important telegrams. Holly Springs with 2000 of our troops had surrendered; hospital and commissary stores burned; my carriage burned and horses captured . . . Before leaving Holly Springs, I was told, some of Van Dorn's staff

officers rode up to the house of which I had lately been an inmate and asked for me. My hostess [Mrs.Govan] assured them I was not there . . . They demanded my baggage, and this also the kind and noble lady protected by her earnest and personal requests.[59]

An account printed in the *Memphis Commercial Appeal* forty years later described the indignant Mrs.

Govan meeting the officers at the head of the stairs and stonily informing them that southern gentlemen didn't invade a lady's bedroom. They retreated. Thus Mrs. Govan had not only saved Mrs. Grant from what she considered a totally inappropriate intrusion, but she probably also saved Walter Place. General Grant issued an order assuring Walter Place's protection for the duration of the war. As Holly Springs seesawed between Union and Confederate occupation, enduring some sixty raids in all, Walter Place was secure and became a favored hiding place for Confederate emissaries.

Harvey Walter (now more commonly called "Colonel Walter") returned home with his family to find Holly Springs devastated. The square had to be rebuilt, railroads refurbished, and overwhelming political and economic problems confronted. Walter devoted himself to steering his adopted hometown through Reconstruction and into the New South, serving as sheriff and as Mississippi's secretary of state. Sensing a promising new business venture, he even organized the Holly Springs Gas & Light Company.

The summer of 1878 found Holly Springs back in flush times. Colonel Walter was an elder statesman of the town and probably concurred with the decision to open the town for those fleeing yellow fever outbreaks in Memphis and Grenada. Mississippi had seen outbreaks of the deadly mosquito-borne scourge at intervals over the previous century, but cases were spread-

Left: Twenty acres of landscaped gardens once surrounded Walter Place.
Right: Walter Place is a unique amalgam of Greek Revival and Gothic Revival elements.

ing that summer at an alarming rate. Ignorant of the disease's vector-based contagiousness, the city fathers of Holly Springs held the assumption that their high elevation (eight hundred feet above sea level) and scarcity of fever cases during past epidemics would render them immune to the infection. Urged on by the generous nature of Harvey Walter, the city rolled out its welcome mat for refugees. The "noble-hearted little city," as it was described in the *New Orleans Times* of August 13, 1878, had sealed its own fate, and nowhere would the grim results be felt more deeply than at Walter Place.

The first refugees arrived by late August, unknowingly carrying the yellow fever virus already. Their symptoms soon appeared and they began to die, but not before salting the local mosquito population with the virus. Holly Springs residents, including Colonel Walter, realized too late the price that their hospitality was going to exact. He hurriedly packed his wife and younger children for evacuation to Huntsville, but refused to go himself. The three oldest Walter sons also remained. Newspaper columnist John Mickle, years later, recalled seeing Colonel Walter going to check on a sick friend. "[He] was much depressed over the situation. 'We are all going to die,' he said, 'but I and my sons will stay.' He turned into the Fort gate and I never saw him again."[60]

Dr. Anne Walter Fearn remembered the loss intently even after sixty years had passed.

A small girl with cropped, curly hair was perched precariously on the edge of the veranda . . . She was being very quiet because she was supposed to be safe inside the house with her three sisters and little brother . . . She watched the townspeople mill around the man on the steps, imploring him to stay with them. She looked up into the man's face and thought of lions, so wonderful were his eyes, so full of power and strength. I was that eleven-year-old child, and the man was my father, Colonel Harvey Washington Walter. That was my last sight of him, standing there with his three grown sons behind him, and telling his neighbors that as long as life lasted he and his sons would remain there with them.[61]

Anne was packed up along with her young siblings and mother and hustled to the depot before the quarantine trapped them in the dying town.

It was all very thrilling to a little girl who liked things to happen, whose mind was stirred by adventure then and always, and who didn't realize the seriousness of that trip or the tragedy left behind. My father and older brothers stayed on, as my father had promised, tending the sick and burying the dead. Our house was turned into a hospital. Every house was in mourning and in many cases whole families were blotted out. But it was not until the first frost had fallen, the greatest danger past, and the end of the epidemic in sight that my father and brothers fell ill with the fever. Then, within one week, all four were dead.[62]

Walter Place had become a house of sorrow. Anne Fearn recalled, "During that long, sad autumn I have fleeting memories of my mother wandering drearily from room to room in the big house which had been so easily filled by the presence of the large-hearted man who was gone. It was years before we heard her laugh again."[63]

Colonel Walter's death put the family in perilous financial straits. The great house was left empty as Anne, her mother, and surviving siblings decamped to the Delta to live with the oldest sister, Minnie, and her husband, Secretary of State Henry Myers. Years would pass with the fate of Walter Place uncertain. It would finally be saved by Colonel Walter's daughter Irene and her husband, Oscar Johnson.

Oscar Johnson was a native of Red Banks, a tiny Marshall County town northwest of Holly Springs. Along with his brother, Jackson, Oscar had made a fortune manufacturing shoes in St. Louis. When Fredonia Walter died, Oscar and Irene took over Walter Place as their summer home. It was then nearly fifty years old and desperately in need of modernization. Oscar brought in famed St. Louis architect Theodore Link, designer of the new Mississippi State Capitol and St. Louis's Union Station, to refurbish the mansion. Bathrooms were squeezed into the octagonal tower rooms. The wrought-iron balcony stretching between the towers was replaced with a more restrained version above the front door. Electricity was installed, and the grand stairway was converted to a double "welcoming-arms" style.

Oscar Johnson wasn't content to merely reshape the house. He envisioned a suburban paradise in the twenty acres surrounding Walter Place. Max Kiern, the landscape architect responsible for St. Louis's Tower Grove Park, was hired and relocated to Holly Springs. He converted the acreage into Johnson Park, with acres of winding trails, formal gardens, Japanese bridges, and lakes. Several antebellum homes included in the park were remodeled and used by the Johnsons as overflow space when they brought trainloads of friends down from St. Louis via private Pullman cars.

Oscar Johnson died in 1916, and his widow sold Walter Place to M. A. Greene, a local Ford dealer. Greene chopped Johnson Park into individual lots, sold them off, and allowed the formal gardens to run wild. Walter Place began to sag. In the 1930s, Anne Walter Fearn, now missionary director of a medical clinic in Shanghai, implored her sister Irene to reacquire the house. At auction on the courthouse steps, deep in the Depression year of 1935, Irene Walter Johnson reclaimed her father's house for four thousand dollars. Another massive renovation was undertaken. The Walter family descendants never really lived there again, and the house was left largely with caretakers for decades. In 1983, it was sold to Mike and Jorja Lynn, who have completely restored it and open it for visitors. Deep within the surrounding woods are the remnants of Johnson Park, and plans are under way to restore it as well.

LONGWOOD

—Natchez

Philadelphian Samuel Sloan published his pattern book for houses, *The Model Architect, Volume II*, in 1852. It established his reputation as one of America's premier architectural innovators and was largely filled with the traditional homes of the day, Gothic villas and Italianate town houses. But readers considering "Design Forty Ninth" were undoubtedly startled at the illustrated plates. On that design, Sloan had pulled out all the stops and let his imagination run wild. Long fascinated with the building arts of Arabia and Constantinople, and borrowing liberally from the eccentric phrenologist Orson Fowler's octagonal theories of energy, Sloan fashioned what he deemed "An Oriental Villa." He freely admitted in the accompanying text that this design was unlikely ever to see the light of day. "It has never, we believe, been chosen for any public building, and there are few instances in which private individuals have selected it for their houses. There are, probably, good reasons why it is not desirable that it should be generally adopted."[64]

The unusual plan gathered dust for almost a decade, until it caught the eye of Haller Nutt, a Natchez millionaire who was independent enough to flaunt the tastes of his neighbors. Greek Revival had dominated the streets and environs of Natchez for thirty years, and Nutt was determined to make his architectural mark in a more flamboyant manner. Had he lived to see it finished, it would have broken his heart to know his house would be forever dubbed "Nutt's Folly."

The landed gentry of antebellum Natchez were the nabobs, second- and third-generation men of wealth and breeding who ruled their town and its social set much as they did their slaves. Haller Nutt was a nabob among nabobs. His father, Rush Nutt, had profited from cotton production and an inventive streak and built Laurel Hill near Rodney. Haller was sent to school in Virginia, and then returned home to Mississippi to claim his fortune. By 1840, he owned several plantations in Mississippi and Louisiana and had married the equally rich and well-connected Julia Williams. Their primary home was at Winter Quarters Plantation, just across the river in Louisiana. In 1850, Nutt bought the old Longwood Mansion and nearly ninety acres surrounding it, just south of Natchez.

The Nutts' two eldest daughters were attending school in Philadelphia. It may have been on a trip to visit them that Haller Nutt first came across the work of Pennsylvania's star architect, Samuel Sloan. For years, Nutt had been considering the possibility of

Left: Interior woodwork of Longwood
Right: Longwood remains an unfinished shell, known to generations of Natchezians as "Nutt's Folly."

tearing down the aging house at Longwood and building his ultimate home on the site. "Design Forty Ninth" in Sloan's book was his choice. Sloan must have been stunned that anyone was going to actually attempt to build this six-story confection. But Nutt was determined and obviously had the resources to follow through; letters began to fly back and forth between Natchez and Philadelphia and on December 24, 1859, Nutt wrote of his intention to start building immediately. Sloan was not going to miss this, the culmination of his wildest creative impulses. He made plans to head south. On January 11, 1860, he wrote to advise Nutt that "I have made all my arrangements to leave for the South on next Tuesday and hope to reach your city one week . . . Our Mr. Greble talks of coming out with me. He has never been South and having time at present thinks he will make the trip."[65] Little did Mr. Sloan and Mr. Greble suspect that in less than a year, Mississippi would be out of the Union and the idea of a business trip to Natchez would be nearly impossible.

Sloan made at least two trips to Natchez in the winter of 1860. Nutt wanted to move quickly. He wrote on March 12, 1860: "I have now moved my family to Natchez—and moving the furniture out of the old house and will in one week from this be ready to take down the old building and commence on the foundation . . . I have now sent down 15 men and 8 boys and will soon commence making bricks."[66] Two weeks

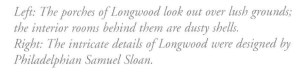

Left: The porches of Longwood look out over lush grounds; the interior rooms behind them are dusty shells.
Right: The intricate details of Longwood were designed by Philadelphian Samuel Sloan.

later, he reported that "I now have my mechanics in the grounds and they are taking down the old house. I am with my family removed to an outbuilding . . ."[67] In early April, he reported again to the architect: "The old house is down and out of the way and the excavation going on though rather slowly. Will be done I hope in 8 or 10 days. Will commence hauling the lumber tomorrow with ten teams."[68] Sloan sent supervisor Addison Hutton and a group of craftsmen to begin work on Longwood.

The Nutts had moved into an impressive three-story servants' quarters just behind the main house site, along with their seven children. They were in the midst of a lush paradise, complete with vast beds of roses and sloping lawns ringed by live oaks and Spanish moss. The house that was beginning to rise before the family's eyes was phenomenal. Slaves were burning 750,000 bricks to compose the twenty-seven-inch-thick walls. Each of the eight sides stretched 37 feet, producing a total circumference of 296 feet. An ingenious system of water pipes were to snake through the walls, carrying rainwater from rooftop reservoirs to inside plumbing and across the grounds to the kitchen. Gas pipes would be laid within the walls, adding a luxurious amenity that only a few Natchez houses could claim. The eventual plans called for six stories, with closets, an office, a smoking room, a playroom, a schoolroom and a billiard room in the basement, formal rooms on the main floor, six bedrooms

on the second floor, and three additional bedrooms on the third floor. Storage space would fill the top levels, and the entire affair would be capped with a huge Moorish dome. Perched on its apex was a twenty-five-foot finial.

Work continued at a frantic pace throughout the summer of 1860, driven as much by fear as by efficiency. Throughout the South, war talk was escalating, and Samuel Sloan's workers were getting worried. In addition to their duties at Longwood, they were remodeling James Alexander Ventress's Woodville farmhouse, LaGrange, into a Greek Revival/Oriental showplace. As conditions deteriorated nationwide at the end of 1860, they grew increasingly restless. The walls of Longwood were nearly complete, but the interior was a vast unfinished shell. Abraham Lincoln had been elected president and South Carolina had bolted from the Union. In January 1861, Mississippi followed. The northern craftsmen saw the writing on the wall. Nutt wrote to Sloan in despair on March 20, 1861: "The bricklayers left on the 16th as I wrote you. On their departure they left without my knowledge a card for a Natchez paper which came out on the 19th and I was much surprised in going into town at everyone knowing it before I did . . . I send you a copy. It will show to Northern people that Philadelphia Mechanics have been South and well treated and not hanged."[69] Under such tense circumstances, the carpenters' note was gracious:

Having terminated the brick work of Mr. Haller Nutt's mansion, we would take this method of tendering to that gentleman our sincere thanks for the very liberal and uniformly kind treatment extended to us during our sojourn with him; and to the citizens of Natchez generally, who have manifested to us the greatest courtesy during the intense excitement through which we have just passed. Signed, Charles Porter, Peter Willets, Wm. L. Room, Oliver Scharz.[70]

These were men who felt they were running for their lives; many probably soon after took up arms against the South, but their hurried departure from Natchez was done with manners intact.

Nutt tried for a few more weeks to smooth the situation over and convince Sloan to send his workers back to Natchez. But the events of Fort Sumter in April and Lincoln's call for troops put an end to his hopes. He wrote Sloan in resignation on May 5: "I wrote you yesterday that there was no danger in sending out men from the North . . . In thinking it over I have thought best to write you again and say that affairs grow more aggrivating [sic] and possibly work men from the North may be molested."[71] Sloan was answering a previous letter on the same day: "The very thought of the condition of our country gives me pain."[72]

The absence of skilled workmen was not the only headache the new war was bringing to Haller Nutt. He was faced with an empty, all but uninhabitable mansion, and the voluminous orders of furniture and accessories were now blockaded. It is uncertain how much of the furniture was ever delivered, or shipped at all. Nutt resigned himself to making do with slave labor through the course of the summer, and in September 1861, the exterior was essentially complete. Inside, the numerous fireplaces were all installed, but only the eight in the basement had mantels. Nutt was in abject despair: "Mr. Smith [one of Sloan's workers] has concluded to leave me and return to his family. I am sorry he does not remain as there is no necessity for his leaving . . . This is perhaps the last chance I may have of writing you until we have Peace returned and I have but little I can write."[73]

There was now no hope of bringing workmen from Philadelphia; those few who had remained on the LaGrange job in Woodville barely escaped, much to Sloan's horror. He informed Nutt of the incident: "It has been rumored that the men have been drove from the work at your house. It is but a rumor and I hope without foundation. We have found it to be a fact that they have been drove from Col. Vantresses [sic] building. One of the workmen wrote from Cincinnati . . . that they barely escaped with their lives and without any cause whatever as they were particularly cautious to avoid everything that would give the slightest reason for molestation."[74]

Nutt supervised his slaves as they finished the basement of the great house. On every level above that

one, empty window frames were boarded over and the cracks between bricks sealed. The front hallway, intended for a "geometrical staircase," was empty and the winds howled down from the clerestory windows of the dome. Haller, Julia, and their children moved into the basement, converting its playroom, office, and smoking room into bedrooms.

Correspondence between Nutt and Sloan still occasionally made it through the battle lines. In October 1863, Sloan wrote what must have been a particularly bitter remark for Nutt to read. "We see no signs of War and in fact were it not for newspapers should not know such was the case."[75] Haller Nutt, on the other hand, knew beyond a doubt that there was a war going on. All the buildings at Winter Quarters except the main house had been destroyed and his crops burned, despite his well-known Unionist sympathies and possession of "protection papers" from Union officers. Lumber and bricks were confiscated from Longwood. Nutt began a fruitless campaign to recover his losses, petitioning the U.S. government for reparations. Julia Nutt was pressed into service as a nurse and hostess. Union wounded were cared for in the house and she later wrote that "Longwood was ever open to hospitality to the United States soldier . . . I do not remember of a single Union officer who visited Natchez during the War who was not the recipient of the hospitalities of Longwood and received there the welcome and comforts of home."[76]

Their hospitality availed them nothing. Haller Nutt sank into a deep depression and wandered the echoing hallways of Longwood. Over the winter of 1863–1864, his health deteriorated. Julia Nutt later wrote of these dark days:

On June 16th, 1864, I buried my husband. He had gone to Vicksburg on private and public business; was much exposed; and taking pneumonia died suddenly. It was not Pneumonia that killed him. The doctor said it was not. It was his troubles. Three million dollars worth of property swept away; the labor of a life time gone; large debts incurred by the War; pressing on him, and his helpless wife with eight children . . . This crushed him and he died. You can give me back my money but you can never give me back my husband nor my children their father and his guiding care.[77]

The Nutts' suit against the federal government would drag on for almost seventy years, eventually leading to recovery of approximately two hundred thousand dollars. Julia raised her children in the dank basement, the only level of the house that was ever completed. During Reconstruction, she rented space out and struggled to survive day to day.

Then came the dark and winter days of my life. I gathered wild weeds and fed my children on them and when winter came on we thanked God when we could get a little corn. My youngest child was but a baby and my oldest son, just sixteen. How we lived God only knows. I cannot recall it all now. But many a time and often in years since then have my children gone to bed half starved and we have lived on sour milk. The world did not know what was going on in my private household and therefore it could not pity us.[78]

Quite possibly, conditions were not so bleak as Julia claimed. Though she never remarried, financial conditions for the family had obviously improved somewhat by 1891, when she sought bids for completion of the house. All were in the eight- to nine-thousand-dollar range and the work was never done. Julia died at Longwood in 1897. Her maiden daughter, also named Julia, lived on there until 1932; at her death, the house passed to the children of Julia and Haller's youngest daughter, Lily Nutt Ward. Merritt Williams Ward, a bachelor, lived there alone until 1939, when it was given over to caretakers. The grounds grew up around it, and all traces of the formal gardens were lost. In 1968, three surviving grandchildren sold the house to the McAdams family of Texas. The McAdams Foundation in turn deeded it to the Pilgrimage Garden Club in 1970. Longwood has been meticulously restored and maintained by the garden club for more than thirty years. Two floors, the finished basement and the partially completed main floor, are open for tours.

Locked doors lead to the ancient wood stairways, spiraling up to chambers that were never used. Wide planks laid on the hardwood provide a safe path through the bricked rooms, covered in fine layers of gray dust. Beautifully arched windows let in light, as well as thousands of wasps that have claimed the interior of the dome as their hive.

Permeating the house is a feeling that time has stood still, forever poised for Samuel Sloan's workmen to return and finish their masterpiece. Longwood will never be completed, as much for symbolic reasons as economic ones. In its stark emptiness, it stands as a constant reminder of a society that rose, prospered, and fell in just a few generations, leaving an architectural legacy that defines antebellum Mississippi for future generations.

{ 140 }

Visitors can still view the unfinished work of Samuel Sloan's carpenters.

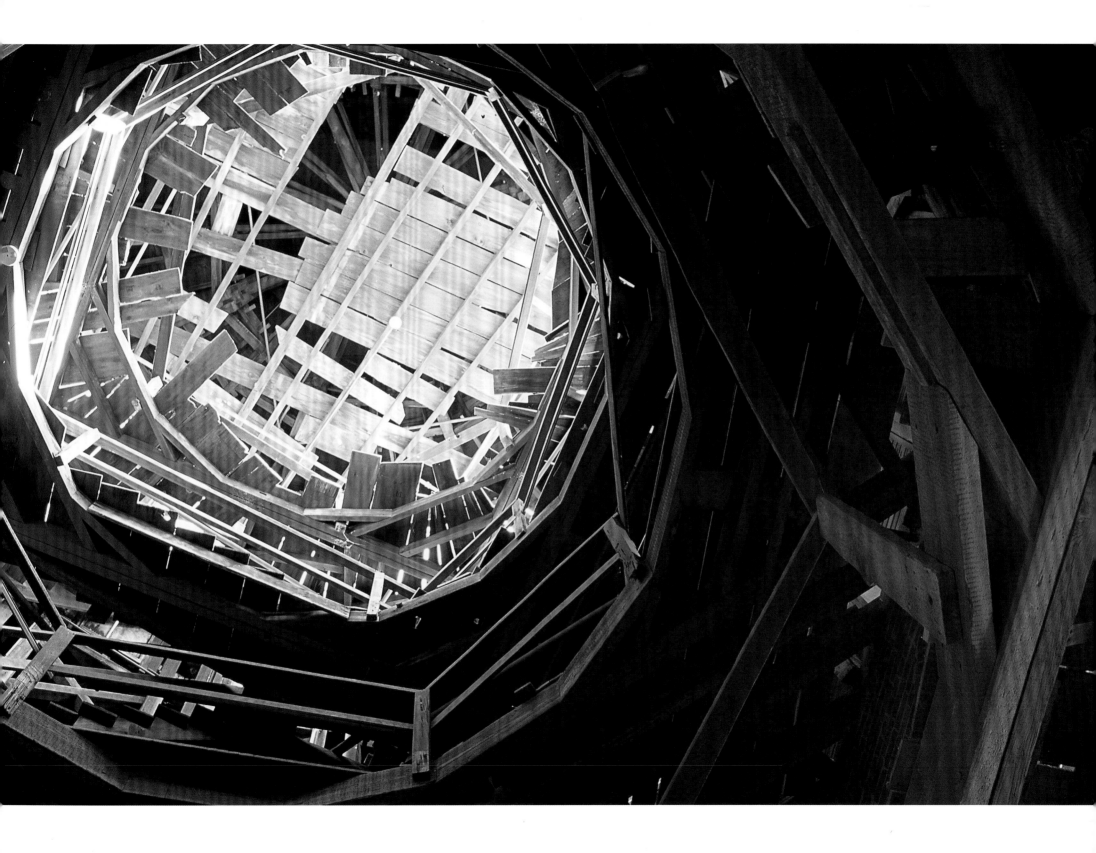

Notes

1. Levi Weeks, as quoted in David King Gleason, photographs, and Mary Warren Miller and Ronald W. Miller, text, *The Great Houses of Natchez* (Jackson: University Press of Mississippi, 1986), 7.

2. Ibid.

3. Norwood Allen Kerr, "The Mississippi Colonization Society (1831–1860)," *Journal of Mississippi History* 43 (1981): 23.

4. Varina Davis, as quoted in Dunbar Rowland, *Mississippi* (1907; reprint, Spartanburg, SC: The Reprint Company, 1976), 1:624.

5. Jefferson Davis, as quoted in *The Papers of Jefferson Davis, Volume I*. Referenced in National Register of Historic Places nomination, Mississippi Department of Archives and History.

6. Quotation from *Morse's Gazette*, in Catharine Van Court, *In Old Natchez* (New York: Doubleday, Doran & Company, 1937), 83.

7. Matilda Gresham, as quoted in Theodora Britton Marshall and Gladys Crail Evans, *They Found It in Natchez* (New Orleans: Pelican Publishing Co., 1939), 163.

8. Advertisement in the *Woodville Republican*, as quoted in *The Journal of Wilkinson County History* 3 (1992): 166.

9. Roger G. Kennedy, *Greek Revival America* (New York: Stewart, Tabori & Chang, 1989), 167.

10. National Register of Historic Places nomination, Mississippi Department of Archives and History.

11. Harnett T. Kane, *Natchez on the Mississippi* (New York: William Morrow and Company, 1947), 283.

12. Mrs. N. D. Deupree, "Some Historic Homes of Mississippi," *Publications of the Mississippi Historical Society* 7 (1903): 326.

13. Sarah Ann Ellis Dorsey, Last Will and Testament, as quoted on Beauvoir Web site, www.beauvoir.org/complete.html.

14. Deupree, "Some Historic Homes of Mississippi," 328.

15. Frazer Smith, *White Pillars: The Architecture of the South* (New York: Bramhall House, 1941), 94–95.

16. *Southern Standard*, November 12, 1852.

17. T. O. Hunter, Jr., as quoted in John Howell Stubbs, "A History of the Tullis House," manuscript in files of Mississippi Department of Archives and History, 10.

18. Deupree, "Some Historic Homes of Mississippi," 340–41.

19. J. W. Clapp, as quoted in Robert Milton Winter, *Memoranda of the Travels of J. W. Clapp* (Franklin, TN: Providence House Publishers, 1997), 188–89.

20. Ibid.

21. Ibid., 341.

22. Robert Milton Winter, *Shadow of a Mighty Rock* (Franklin: Providence House Publishers, 1997), 484.

23. Mary Howey Key, interview by Roberta Miller, Mississippi Department of Archives and History and Washington County Library System Oral History Project (October 1977).

24. Charles Dahlgren, quoted in *The Daily Democrat*, January 24, 1886.

25. Advertisement in *Natchez Daily Courier*, March 25, 1858.

26. Quotation from the *Oxford Falcon*, November 23, 1865.

27. Kane, *Natchez on the Mississippi*, 286.

28. National Register of Historic Places nomination, Mississippi Department of Archives and History.

29. Hugh Miller Thompson II, *The Johnstones of Annandale* (privately printed, 1992), 22–24.

30. Andrew Jackson Downing, *The Architecture of Country Houses* (1850; reprint, New York: Dover Publications, 1969), 257–58.

31. Samuel Sloan, *The Model Architect, Volume II* (1852; reprint, New York: DeCapo Press, 1975), 31–32.

32. Mrs. Harris Barksdale, *Holland's*, June 1936, 26.

33. Hinkle, Guild & Company catalogue, 1862 edition, 54.

34. Will of John Williams Boddie, recorded in Madison County Chancery Clerk's office, Book 8, 394.

35. Kate Power in unidentified November 1895 newspaper.

36. Downing, *Architecture of Country Houses*, 295.

37. Quotation by unidentified writer from December 12, 1888, *New Mississippian*.

38. Alexander Bondurant, "Sherwood Bonner: Her Life and Place in the Literature of the South," *Publications of the Mississippi Historical Society* 1 (1898): 45.

39. Sherwood Bonner, as quoted in Hubert H. McAlexander, *The Prodigal Daughter: A Biography of Sherwood Bonner* (Baton Rouge: LSU Press, 1981), 8.

40. Ibid., 12.

41. Ibid., 15.

42. Ibid., 16.

{ 144 }

43. Ibid., 117.

44. Ibid., 117.

45. Ibid., 142.

46. Ibid., 16.

47. Helen Craft Anderson, as quoted in McAlexander, *Prodigal Daughter*, 209–10.

48. John Mickle, *South Reporter*, August 7, 1930.

49. Mildred Strickland, as quoted in Robert Milton Winter, ed., *Civil War Women* (Lafayette, CA: Thomas Berryhill Press, 2001), 259.

50. John Y. Simon, ed., *The Personal Memoirs of Julia Dent Grant (Mrs. Ulysses S. Grant)* (Carbondale: Southern Illinois University Press, 1975), 109.

51. Ibid.

52. Olga Reed Pruitt, *It Happened Here: True Stories of Holly Springs* (1950; reprint, Holly Springs: Marshall County Historical Society, 1998), 61.

53. Mickle, *South Reporter*.

54. George Stephenson, "The Day Caruso Died," as quoted in Chesley Thorne Smith, *Childhood in Holly Springs* (Lafayette, CA: Thomas Berryhill Press, 1996), 112–13.

55. Robert Snow, as quoted in Heath Childs, *Waverley: Memories of a Mississippi Plantation* (Columbus: Higginbotham's Southern Printing, 2000), 53.

56. Ibid., 55.

57. *Goodspeed's Biographical and Historical Memoirs of Mississippi* (Chicago: Goodspeed, 1891).

58. Simon, ed., *Personal Memoirs of Julia Dent Grant*, 105.

59. Ibid., 107.

60. John Mickle, as quoted in Hubert H. McAlexander, *A Southern Tapestry* (Virginia Beach, VA: The Donning Company, 2000), 71.

61. Anne Walter Fearn, *My Days of Strength* (New York: Harper & Brothers, 1939), 1.

62. Ibid., 2.

63. Ibid., 3.

64. Samuel Sloan, as quoted in Ina McAdams, *The Building of Longwood* (privately printed, 1992), 1.

65. Ibid., 10.

66. Haller Nutt, as quoted in McAdams, *Building of Longwood*, 23.

67. Ibid., 29.

68. Ibid., 35.

69. Ibid., 63.

70. Ibid., 64.

71. Ibid., 65.

72. Sloan, as quoted in McAdams, *Building of Longwood*, 68.

73. Nutt, as quoted in McAdams, *Building of Longwood*, 81.

74. Sloan, as quoted in McAdams, *Building of Longwood*, 83.

75. Ibid., 92.

76. Julia Nutt, as quoted in McAdams, *Building of Longwood*, 115.

77. Ibid., 115–16.

78. Ibid., 116.

Bibliography

Anderson, Helen Craft. "A Chapter in the Yellow Fever Epidemic of 1878." *Publications of the Mississippi Historical Society* 10 (1909): 223–36.

Bagley, Clinton. Remarks at presentation of Mount Holly historical marker, October 10, 1998.

Barksdale, Mrs. Harris. "Distinctive Gardens: The Rucker Garden at Canton, Mississippi." *Holland's*, June 1936, 26.

Bergeron, Kat. "Tullis-Toledano Manor Maintains Its Regal Beauty Through the Years." Biloxi *Sun-Herald*, n.d.

Bertram, Jack. "Saving Riverview." Jackson *Clarion-Ledger*, February 2, 2001.

Boddie, John Bennett. *Boddie and Allied Families*. Unpublished manuscript in collection of Mississippi Department of Archives and History, n.d.

Bondurant, Alexander L. "Sherwood Bonner: Her Life and Place in the Literature of the South." *Publications of the Mississippi Historical Society* 1 (1898): 43–68.

Branson, Reed. "Belmont Plantation Primed for Sale." *Commercial Appeal*, July 17, 2000.

Campbell, Clarice T. "Exploring the Roots of Tougaloo College." *Journal of Mississippi History* 35 (February 1973): 15–28.

Carpenter, Edwina. "Walter Place: Residence of Grant During Occupation of Holly Springs." *South Reporter*, April 24, 1986.

Childs, Heath. *Waverley: Memories of a Mississippi Plantation*. Columbus: Higginbotham's Southern Printing, 2000.

Cooledge, Harold N., Jr. *Samuel Sloan: Architect of Philadelphia, 1815–1884*. Philadelphia: University of Pennsylvania Press, 1986.

Cooper, J. Wesley. *Antebellum Houses of Natchez*. Natchez: Southern Historical Publications, 1970.

Cooper, William C., Jr. *Jefferson Davis, American*. New York: Alfred A. Knopf, 2000.

Crocker, Mary Wallace. *Historic Architecture in Mississippi*. Jackson: University Press of Mississippi, 1973.

Davis, William C. *Jefferson Davis: The Man and His Hour*. New York: Harper Collins, 1991.

Deupree, J. G. "The Capture of Holly Springs, Mississippi, December 20, 1862." *Publications of the Mississippi Historical Society* 4 (1901): 49–61.

Deupree, Mrs. N. D. "Some Historic Homes of Mississippi." *Publications of the Mississippi Historical Society* 7 (1903): 325–47.

Douglas, Ed Polk. *Architecture in Claiborne County, Mississippi: A Selective Guide*. Jackson: Mississippi Department of Archives and History, 1974.

Downing, A. J. *The Architecture of Country Houses*. 1850. Reprint, New York: Dover Publications, 1969.

Doyle, Don H. *Faulkner's County: The Historical Roots of Yoknapatawpha*. Chapel Hill: University of North Carolina Press, 2001.

Duval, Paul. "Cedar Grove, A Man's Monument." Manuscript in collection of Mississippi Department of Archives and History.

Evans, Patricia E. *West Family Genealogical Records*. Unpublished manuscript, n.d.

Fearn, Anne Walter. *My Days of Strength*. New York: Harper & Brothers, 1939.

Gandy, Joan, and Thomas Gandy. *Natchez: Landmarks, Lifestyle and Leisure*. Charleston: Arcadia Press, 1999.

Gleason, David King, photographs, and Mary Warren Miller and Ronald W. Miller, text. *The Great Houses of Natchez*. Jackson: University Press of Mississippi, 1986.

Gower, Herschel. *Charles Dahlgren of Natchez*. Washington, D.C.: Brassey's, Inc., 2002.

Harrell, Virginia C. *Vicksburg and the River*. Vicksburg: Harrell Publications, 1986.

Haynes, Jane Isbell. *William Faulkner: His Lafayette County Heritage*. Columbia: Seajay Society, 1992.

Hines, Thomas. *William Faulkner and the Tangible Past: The Architecture of Yoknapatawpha*. Berkeley: University of California Press, 1996.

Howell, Elmo. *Mississippi Home-Places*. N.p., n.d.

James, D. Clayton. *Antebellum Natchez*. 1968. Reprint, Baton Rouge: LSU Press, 1993.

Jones, Marilyn, and Jean Schott. *Manship House Museum*. Lawrenceburg: The Creative Company, 1998.

Kennedy, Roger G. *Greek Revival America*. New York: Stewart, Tabori & Chang, 1989.

Kane, Harnett T. *Natchez on the Mississippi*. New York: William Morrow and Company, 1947.

Kerr, Norwood Allen. "The Mississippi Colonization Society (1831–1860)." *Journal of Mississippi History* 43 (February 1981): 1–30.

Lafoe, Lynn. "Mount Holly." *Delta Democrat Times*, October 4, 1998.

Lane, Mills. *Architecture of the Old South: Mississippi/Alabama.* New York: Abbeville Press, 1989.

Lawrence, John, and Dan Hise. *Faulkner's Rowan Oak.* Jackson: University Press of Mississippi, 1993.

Lewis, John. "Woodville Home Built in 1832 Gutted by Fire." *Woodville Republican,* July 23, 1998.

Marshall, Theodora Britton, and Gladys Crail Evans. *They Found It in Natchez.* New Orleans: Pelican Publishing Company, 1939.

May, Robert E. *John A. Quitman: Old South Crusader.* Baton Rouge: LSU Press, 1985.

McAdams, Ina May Ogletree. *The Building of Longwood.* N.p., 1972.

McAlester, Virginia, and Lee McAlester. *A Field Guide to American Houses.* New York: Alfred A. Knopf, 1986.

McAlexander, Hubert H. *The Prodigal Daughter: A Biography of Sherwood Bonner.* Baton Rouge: LSU Press, 1981.

———. *A Southern Tapestry: Marshall County, Mississippi, 1835–2000.* Virginia Beach: The Donning Company, 2000.

McIntire, Carl. "More on Mount Holly." Jackson *Clarion-Ledger,* February 18, 1973.

McIntosh, James T. *The Papers of Jefferson Davis.* Vol 1. Baton Rouge: LSU Press, 1974.

Mead, Carol Lynn. *The Land Between Two Rivers.* Canton: Friends of the Madison County Public Library, 1987.

Mickle, John. *South Reporter,* August 7, 1930.

Mullen, Phil. "Grand Old Fulton House Little Changed in 120 Years." *Madison County Herald,* 20 November 1958.

Pitts, Stella. "Feltus-Catchings House." *Journal of Wilkinson County History* 3 (November 1992): 164–67.

Polk, Noel, ed. *Natchez Before 1830.* Jackson: University Press of Mississippi, 1989.

Powell, Mary Ellen. "Several Lifetimes All Rolled Into One." *Delta Business Journal,* May 2, 2000.

P'Pool, Kenneth H. "The Architectural History of a Mississippi Town 1817–1866." Unpublished manuscript, 1990.

Pray, Brian. "State Certified Appraisal Report of an Historic Antebellum Mansion Known as Neilson-Culley House." Unpublished manuscript located in files of Mississippi Department of Archives and History.

Pruitt, Olga Reed. *It Happened Here: True Stories of Holly Springs.* 1950. Reprint, Holly Springs: Marshall County Historical Society, 1998.

Pryor, David. "Cedarhurst: Home of Sherwood Bonner." *South Reporter,* April 22, 1982.

Rosenblum, Thom. *John McMurran of Melrose.* National Park Service Publishing, 2001.

Rowland, Dunbar. *Mississippi.* 1907. Reprint, Spartanburg, SC: The Reprint Company, 1976.

Rybczynski, Witold. *A Clearing in the Distance.* New York: Scribner, 1999.

Sansing, David G., Sim C. Callon, and Carolyn Vance Smith. *Natchez: An Illustrated History.* Natchez: Plantation Publishing Company, 1992.

Simon, John Y. "In Search of Margaret Johnson Erwin: A Research Note." *Journal of American History* 69 (March 1983): 932.

———, ed. *The Personal Memoirs of Julia Dent Grant (Mrs. Ulysses S. Grant).* Carbondale: Southern Illinois University Press, 1975.

Smith, J. Frazer. *White Pillars: The Architecture of the South.* New York: Bramhall House, 1941.

Stephenson, George. "The Day Caruso Died." Chapter in Chesley Thorne Smith, *Childhood in Holly Springs.* Lafayette, CA: Thomas Berryhill Press, 1996.

Stubbs, John Howell. "A History of the Tullis House." Manuscript located in files of Mississippi Department of Archives and History.

Van Court, Catharine. *In Old Natchez.* New York: Doubleday, Doran & Company, 1937.

Watkins, Ruth. "Reconstruction in Marshall County." *Publications of the Mississippi Historical Society* 12 (1912): 155–213.

Webb, Walter. "Airliewood." *South Reporter,* n.d.

Wells, Dean Faulkner. *The Ghosts of Rowan Oak.* Oxford: Yoknapatawpha Press, 1980.

Whitwell, William L. *The Heritage of Longwood.* Jackson: University Press of Mississippi, 1975.

Williamson, Joel. *William Faulkner and Southern History.* New York: Oxford University Press, 1993.

Wilson, Jack Case. *Faulkners, Fortunes and Flames.* Nashville: Annandale Press, 1984.

Winter, Robert Milton. *Memoranda of the Travels of J. W. Clapp.* Franklin, TN: Providence House Publishers, 1997.

———. *Shadow of a Mighty Rock.* Franklin: Providence House Publishers, 1997.

———, ed. *Our Pen Is Time: The Diary of Emma Finley.* Lafayette, CA: Thomas Berryhill Press, 1999.

———, ed. *Civil War Women: The Diaries of Belle Strickland and Cora Harris Watson.* Lafayette, CA: Thomas Berryhill Press, 2001.

Works Progress Administration. *Mississippi: The WPA Guide to the Magnolia State.* 1938. Reprint, Jackson: University Press of Mississippi, 1988.

Wright, Holly. "Historic Gates at Coxe-Dean Home Restored." *South Reporter,* September 9, 1999.

Index

References to illustrations appear in *italics*.

Adam brothers, architectural influence of, 1

Agricultural Bank (Natchez), 24

Airliewood, 107, *113, 114, 116*; built by W. H. Coxe, 113; description, 101, 113, 115; porch alterations, 117; sold to D. C. Topp, 117; use as hospital, 117

Aldemar, crumbles into Mississippi River, 97

American Colonization Society. *See* Mississippi Colonization Society

Ammadelle, 82, *93, 94, 95, 96*; built by William Turner for Thomas Pegues, 93; description, 95; designed by Calvert Vaux, 93; renamed, 95; sale to subsequent owners, 95; torched during Civil War, 95

Anchuca, xiv

Annandale, xiv, 81, 90

Arlington, xiv, 3

Athenia, xiii, xiv, 26, 57, *57, 58, 59, 59*, 107; built by W. W. Clapp, 57; during Civil War, 59; sold to A. M. West, 60; subsequent owners, 60

Auburn, xiv, *7, 8, 9*; bought by Stephen Duncan, 10; built by Levi Weeks for Lyman Harding, 7; left to city of Natchez, 10

Balfour House, xiv

Beauvoir, *44, 45, 46*; built by James Brown, 44; conversion to veterans' home, 47; description, 44; sale to Jefferson Davis, 47;

sale to Sarah Dorsey, 46; site of Confederate reunions, 47; use by Jefferson Davis, 46

Belfast. *See* Stanton Hall

Belmont, *65, 67*; built by William Worthington, 64; description, 64, 66; use as hunting club, 66

Benjamin, Asher, as author of design books, 25

Boddie, John Williams: builds Boddie Mansion, 90; family lore, 90; moves to Mississippi, 90; will, 92

Boddie Mansion, 82, *91*; bought by American Missionary Association, 92; built by J. W. Boddie, 90; decline and renovation, 92; inclusion in Hinkle, Guild & Company catalogue, 90; use by Tougaloo College, 92; use during Civil War, 92

Boling, Spires, xiv, 26, 125; builds Walter Place, 127, 128

Bondurant, Alexander, on Sherwood Bonner, 108

Bonner, Charles: builds home in Holly Springs, 107; children, 107; Civil War service and role in Reconstruction, 110; marries Mary Wilson, 107; moves to Mississippi, 107

Bonner, Katherine Sherwood, 107; childhood, 108; description of Holly Springs during Civil War, 110; description of yellow fever epidemic, 111; divorce, 112; illness and death, 112; marriage, 111; relationship with Henry W. Longfellow, 111

Bonner, Martha, 111, 112

Boyd, Alexander: builds Magnolia Hill, 29; death, 29

Briars, 3

Brown, Fredonia: life at Walter Place, 132; marries Harvey Washington Walter, 127

Brown, James, builds Beauvoir, 44

Camellia Place, xiv

Carmichael, John, xiii; army career, 4; builds Cold Spring, 4; death, 4

Carter-Tate House, 73, 74

Catchings, Charles, buys Feltus-Catchings House, 17

Cedar Grove, xiv, *31, 32, 33*; built by W. A. Klein, 31; damage during Civil War, 31, 32; gardens, 33; Italianate elements, 82; subsequent owners, 33

Cedarhurst, 101, *107, 108, 109, 110*; auctioned, 112; built by Charles Bonner, 107; during Civil War, 110, 111; description, 108, 110; location, 107; during Reconstruction, 111; sold to Belk family, 112; during yellow fever epidemic, 111

Cherokee, 43, 76

Choctaw, 43

Clapp, W. W.: builds Athenia, 57; career in Holly Springs, 57; during Civil War, 59; involvement with Mississippi Central Railroad, 57; sells house to A. M. West, 60

Clapp-Fant House. *See* Athenia

Clifton, 3

Cold Spring, *5, 6*; built by John Carmichael, 4; description, 4; legends, 6; as one of state's oldest houses, xiii; setting, 4; sold to McGehee family, 6

Columbus Eclectic Style, xiv, 26, 101, 125

Concord, xiv, 2; inherited by George Malin Davis Kelly, 43

{ 148 }

Coxe, Amelia, 113, 115

Coxe, Lida Victoria, 113, 115

Coxe, William Henry: builds Airliewood, 113; death, 117; as remembered by Julia Grant, 115

Dahlgren, Charles, xiii; builds Dunleith, 70; loses Routhlands to fire, 70; marries Mary Ellis Routh, 70; moves to Natchez, 70

Daniell, Smith Coffee, xiii, 26

Darrington, John, 3

Davis, Alexander Jackson, as designer of Gothic Revival houses, 101

Davis, Ebenezer Nelms: attacked by Union soldiers, 61; builds Strawberry Plains, 61; partially restores Strawberry Plains, 61

Davis, George, buys Melrose, 43

Davis, Jane: death, 12; plants roses at Rosemont, 12

Davis, Jefferson: childhood at Rosemont, 12; death, 47; election as Confederate president, 11; partial payments on Beauvoir, 47; post–Civil War career, 46; writes memoirs at Beauvoir, 46

Davis, Joseph, saves Rosemont from foreclosure, 12

Davis, Martha, during Civil War at Strawberry Plains, 61

Davis, Samuel Emory: builds Rosemont, 11; death, 12; loses title to house, 12; moves family to Mississippi, 11

Davis, Varina Howell, 11; inherits Beauvoir, 47; marriage to Jefferson Davis, 12; moves to Beauvoir, 46; sale of house to Sons of Confederate Veterans, 47

D'evereux, xiv

Dorsey, Sarah Ellis: buys Beauvoir, 46; relationship with Jefferson Davis, 46; will, 46

Downing, Andrew Jackson, 83, 101; association with Gothic Revival style, 113; association with Calvert Vaux, 93; death, 93; as designer of Italianate houses, 81

Duff Green House, xiv

Duncan, Stephen: buys Auburn, 10; career as physician and planter, 10; death, 10; enlarges Auburn, 10; leaves Mississippi, 10; marriages, 10; role in Mississippi Colonization Society, 10

Dunleith, xiv, 24, *71, 72*; built by Charles Dahlgren, 70; description, 70, 72; subsequent owners, 72

Eclectic architecture, xiv, 119. *See also* Longwood; Walter Place; Waverley; White Arches

Edgecomb. *See* Ammadelle

Edgewood, 82

Elliott, Fannie, opens hospital at Airliewood, 117

Erwin, Margaret Johnson: builds Mount Holly, 97; marries James Erwin, 97

Fant, Lester G., buys Athenia, 60

Faulkner, William: buys Rowan Oak, 39; death, 39; uses local houses in novels, 74, 96; writing career, 39

Fearn, Anne Walter, 132; urges sister to reacquire Walter Place, 133

Federal style architecture, xiv, 3, 24. *See also* Auburn; Cold Spring; Feltus-Catchings House; Lewis House; Rosalie; Rosemont

Feltus, Abram M.: built by Abram Scott, 17; buys house from Prestwood Smith, 17; career, 17

Feltus-Catchings House, xiii, *18*; description, 17; subsequent owners, 17; use as boardinghouse, 17

Finley, Ruth, wills Strawberry Plains to Audubon Society, 63

Finley, Thomas, buys Strawberry Plains, 63

Forest, The, 3, 70

Forks of Cypress (Alabama), 70

Fort Panmure. *See* Fort Rosalie

Fort Rosalie: destruction, 15; site chosen by Bienville, 15

French/West Indian style architecture, xiv, 2

Fulton, David Matthew: builds dogtrot house, 86; death, 88; enlarges home, 86; losses during Civil War, 86; moves to Canton, 86; problems during Reconstruction, 88

Fulton House. *See* Wohlden

Galena, 113

Gemmell, Peter, architect of Ravenna, 25

Gibbons, William: as architect of Greek Revival buildings, 24; builds Jackson City Hall, 24; work on Mississippi State Lunatic Asylum, 24

Gilruth, I. N., buys Wilson House, 35

Glenwood, 26

Gloucester, xiv

Goat Castle. *See* Glenwood

Gothic Revival style architecture, xiv, 101. *See also* Airliewood; Cedarhurst; Manship House

Govan, Mary, life at Walter Place during Civil War, 128, 131

Grant, Jesse, son of Ulysses and Julia Grant, 115

Grant, Julia: life at Airliewood, 115; life at Rosalie, 16; life at Walter Place, 131

Grant, Ulysses: occupies Rosalie, 16, 115; occupies Walter Place, 128

Greek Revival style architecture, xiv, 23, 24, 26. *See also* Athenia; Beauvoir; Belmont; Cedar Grove; Dunleith; Magnolia Hill; Magnolias, The; Martha Vick House; Melrose; Mosby Home; Neilson-Culley-Lewis; Riverview; Rowan Oak; Stanton Hall; Strawberry Plains; Tullis-Toledano Manor; Wilson-Gilruth House

Greenwood Plantation (Louisiana), 70

Gresham, Walter Q., occupies Rosalie, 16

Griffin, James S., designs Rosalie, 15

Harding, Lyman, 10; to build Auburn, 7; career in Natchez, 7

Harris, Jeptha Vining, builds White Arches, 125

Holliday Haven, 49

Homewood, xiv

House on Ellicott Hill, xiv, 2

Hoyt, Ep, 7

Hoyt, T. J., as architect of The Burn, 25

Ingleside, xiv, 81

Italianate style architecture, xiv, 81. *See also* Ammadelle; Boddie Mansion; Mount Holly; Rosedale; Wohlden

Jackson City Hall, 24

Johnson, Henry, as early landowner in Mississippi Delta, 97

Johnson, Irene: buys Walter Place at auction, 133; restores Walter Place, 132

Johnson, Oscar: builds Johnson Park, 133; hires Theodore Link as architect, 132; restores Walter Place, 132

Johnson, Solie, and gardens at Wohlden, 88

Johnson Park, description, 133

Johnstone, Margaret, builds Annandale, 81

Kelly, George Malin Davis, inherits four Natchez mansions, 43

Kennedy, Roger, 23

King, Caleb, founds Kingston, 29

Klein, William Alexander: builds Cedar Grove, 31; builds sawmills, 31; during Civil War, 32; death, 33; marries Elizabeth Day, 31; moves to Vicksburg, 31; during Reconstruction, 33

Klein, William Tecumseh Sherman, born during Vicksburg Seige, 33; death, 33

Lafever, Minard, 25

Lane, John, lays out Vicksburg grid, 27

Larmour, Jacob, architectural designs, 90

LeGrande, Jules, paints murals at Tullis-Toledano Manor, 54

L'enfant, Pierre, 1

Leota, collapses into Mississippi River, 64

Lewis, John S.: buys Woodville *Republican*, 19; inherits Lewis House, 19

Lewis House, *19, 21*; built by Thomas Lynne, 20; as depicted in WPA photos, 20; description, 20; fire and restoration, 21

Linden, xiv, 3

Link, Theodore, as architect for Walter Place restoration, 132

Little, Eliza Low, marries Peter Little, 15

Little, Peter: builds Parsonage, 16; builds Rosalie, 15; builds sawmill, 15; death, 16; early years in Natchez, 15; marries Eliza Low, 15

Longfellow, Henry Wadsworth, relationship with Sherwood Bonner, 111

Longwood, xiii, 119, *134, 135, 136, 141*; basis of design, 134; completion considered, 140; construction begins, 137; description, 138; inherited by Nutt children and grandchildren, 140; loss of workers, 138; losses to Union troops, 139; original house demolished, 137; post–Civil War, 139; sold to McAdams Foundation, 140; as symbol of architectural decline, xv, 119; transfer to Pilgrimage Garden Club, 140; visit by Samuel Sloan, 137

Lull, James, as Columbus architect, 51

Lynne, Thomas: builds Lewis House, 19; sells house to John South Lewis, 19

Lyons, Wiley, builds Mosby Home, 68

Magnolia Hill, xiv, *30*; built by Alexander Boyd, 29; description, 29; outbuildings, 29; subsequent owners, 29

Magnolias, The, xiv, *48*; built by William A. Sykes, 49; description, 49; donation to city of Aberdeen, 49; renovation, 49; unusual stairway, 49

Manship, Adaline: during Civil War, 105; marriage to Charles Manship, 102; wedding anniversary, 106

Manship, Charles Henry: builds Manship House, 105; death, 106; early career, 102; moves to Mississippi, 102; newspaper ad, 102; serves as mayor of Jackson, 105; wedding anniversary celebration, 106

Manship House, xiv, *102, 103, 104*; built by Charles Manship, 105; during Civil War, 105; description, 105; renovation by Mississippi Department of Archives and History, 106

Martha Vick House, *28*; built by Martha Vick, 27; description, 28; subsequent owners, 28

Martin, John D.: sells land to Robert Sheegog, 37

McDowell, Lilian, 111, 112

McLaran, Charles: builds Riverview, 51; moves to Columbus, 51

McMurran, John T.: builds Melrose, 40; death, 43; financial struggles, 42; marries Mary Louisa Turner, 40; moves to Natchez, 40; partnership with John A. Quitman, 40; sells Melrose, 43

Melrose, xiii, *41, 42*; built by John McMurran, 40; during Civil War, 42; decline and restoration, 43; description, 40, 42; sale to George Davis, 43; sale to National Park Service, 43

Mississippi Central Railroad, started by Holly Springs investors, 57

Mississippi Colonization Society, 10

Mississippi State Lunatic Asylum, 24

Montrose, xiv, 26, 57, 107

Mosby Home, *69*; built by Wiley Lyons, 68; bought by Mosby family, 68; description, 68

Mount Holly, 82, *98*; built by Margaret J. Erwin, 97; description, 99; subsequent owners, 99

Mount Repose, xiv

Murphree, Dennis, buys Belmont for hunting club, 66

Natchez Masonic Hall, 3

Natchez National Historic Park, includes Melrose, 40

Neibert, Joseph, as architect of Ravenna, 25

Neilson, Ed: Civil War incident, 74; rebuilds mercantile store, 74

Neilson, William: builds home, 73; involvement in Civil War, 73; moves to Oxford, 73; opens mercantile store, 73

Neilson-Culley-Lewis House, *73, 75*; built by William Neilson, 73; during Civil War, 73, 74; description, 73; possible model for Faulkner story, 74; subsequent owners, 74

Nichols, William, architect of Old Capitol, Lyceum and Governor's Mansion, 24

Nutt, Haller, xiii, xv, 119; contracts with Samuel Sloan, 134; correspondence regarding Longwood, 137, 138, 139; death, 139; early landholdings, 134; finishes basement, 139; moves family to Longwood site, 138

Nutt, Julia: death, 140; letters to government regarding Longwood, 139; solicits bids for completion of house, 140

Nutt's Folly. *See* Longwood

Octagonal style architecture, 119

Oriental style architecture, 119

Pain, William, as author of design book, 2, 10

Palladio, Andrea, role in development of classical architecture, 1, 23

Pegues, Thomas: builds Edgecomb (Ammadelle), 95; contracts

{ 150 }

with Calvert Vaux for house design, 93; moves to Oxford, 93; plants trees along North (Lamar) Avenue, 93

Pointer Mansion, 57

Poplar Grove. *See* Rosemont

Price, Bem, buys Edgecomb and changes name to Ammadelle, 95

Prospect Hill Plantation, 10

Quitman, John Anthony, becomes John McMurran's partner, 40

Ravenna, 25

Rittlemeyer brothers, work on Airliewood, 113

Riverview, xiii, xiv, 26, *50, 51, 52, 53*; built by Charles McLaran, 51; description, 51, 52, 53; deterioration and near-demolition, 53; renovation, 53; subsequent owners, 53

Rosalie, xiv, *14*; built by Peter Little, 15; during Civil War, 16; description, 3, 15, 16; restoration by DAR, 16; sale to Wilson family, 16

Rosedale, xiv, 82, *85*; built by W. W. Topp, 84; description, 83, 84; possible connection with Samuel Sloan, 83

Rosemont, xiii, *11, 13*; built by Samuel Davis, 11; description, 11, 12; restoration, 12; subsequent owners, 12

Rose, Thomas, as architect of Stanton Hall, 76

Ross, Isaac, attempts to free slaves through will, 10

Routh, Job, builds Routhlands, 70

Routhlands, 26; destroyed by fire, 70; remaining outbuildings, 70

Rowan Oak, *37, 38*; built by Robert Sheegog, 37; bought and renovated by William Faulkner, 38; during Civil War, 37; description, 37; subsequent owners, 37

Rucker, Edward, inherits Fulton House (Wohlden), 88

Rucker, Maria, inherits Fulton House (Wohlden), 88

Salisbury, 4

Scott, Abram, 19; builds house in Woodville (Feltus-Catchings House), 17; death, 17; serves as governor, 17

Shackleford, John, restores Strawberry Plains, 63

Shackleford, Margaret Finley, restores Strawberry Plains, 63

Sheegog, Robert R.: accumulates large landholdings, 37; builds home in Oxford, 37; death, 37

Sheegog House. *See* Rowan Oak

Sieur de Bienville, chooses sight for Fort Rosalie, 15

Sloan, Samuel, xv, 83, 84, 119; association with Haller Nutt, 134; designs Longwood, 134; letters to Nutt, 138

Smith, Frazer, renovates the Magnolias, 49

Smith, Prestwood: buys Feltus-Catchings House, 17; murdered, 17

Snow, Donna, buys and restores Waverley, 124

Snow, Robert, 124; buys and restores Waverley quotation, 124

Stanton, Frederick, xiii, 26; builds Stanton Hall, 76; career as cotton broker, 76; death, 78; furnishes house, 78

Stanton Hall, xiii, 24, *76, 77, 79*; built by Frederick Stanton, 76; during Civil War, 78; description, 78; deterioration, 78; restoration by Pilgrimage Garden Club, 78; sold for use as school, 78

Strawberry Plains, xiv, *62, 63*; built by Ebenezer Davis, 61; burned during Civil War, 61; donation to Audubon Society, 63; renovation, 63

Swan, Abraham, as author of design book, 2, 8

Swayze, Richard, settles near Natchez, 29

Swayze, Samuel, settles near Natchez, 29

Swiftwater, 82

Sykes, William Alfred, builds the Magnolias, 49

Thomas, Frances, rescues and renovates Riverview, 53

Thompson, Jacob, home burned by Union troops, 73

Toledano, Christoval Sebastian: builds Tullis-Toledano Manor, 54; death, 54; marries Matilde Pradat, 54; moves to Biloxi, 54

Topp, Dixon Comfort, buys Airliewood, 117

Topp, W. W., builds Rosedale, 84

Tullis, Garner, renovates Tullis-Toledano Manor, 56

Tullis-Toledano Manor, *55*; built by Christoval Toledano, 54; damaged during Hurricane Camille, 56; description, 54; LeGrande murals and their destruction, 54, 56; sold to city of Biloxi, 56; subsequent owners, 54

Turner, William, 26; builds Edgecomb (Ammadelle), 93; builds Neilson-Culley-Lewis House, 73

Uncle Sam Plantation (Louisiana), 70

Vaux, Calvert, 82; draws designs for Edgecomb (Ammadelle), 93; works with Frederick Law Olmsted on Central Park, 93

Ventress, James Alexander, 138; hires Samuel Sloan's workers from Longwood, 26

Vick, Henry William, 27

Vick, John Wesley, 27

Vick, Martha: business acumen, 27; builds house, 27; death, 28; death of parents, 27; education, 27

Wakefield, 26, 57, 107

Wall House, 4

Walnut Hills. *See* Vicksburg

Walpole, Horace, 101

Walter, Harvey Washington: during Civil War, 130; connections with Mississippi Central Railroad, 128; death, 132; early career, 127; moves to Holly Springs, 127; marries Fredonia Brown, 127; role in Reconstruction, 131; role in yellow fever epidemic, 131, 132

Walter Place, xiv, 26, 101, 119, *127, 128, 129, 130, 131*; built by Harvey W. Walter, 128; during Civil War, 129; closed up by family, 132; description, 129; development of formal gardens, 133; modernized by Theodore Link, 132; sold at auction, 133; subsequent owners and renovations, 133; during yellow fever epidemic, 131, 132

Waverley, xiv, xv, 21, *119, 121, 122*; abandonment and restoration 124; built by George Hampton Young, 123; description, 123; outbuildings, 123; ventilation system, 123

Wayside, 64

Weeks, Levi: arrives in Natchez, 2; builds Auburn for Lyman Harding, 2; death, 60; nomination for vice-presidency, 60; other building projects in Mississippi, 2, 60

Weldon brothers: employ African-American draftsman, 25; work on Warren and Hinds county courthouses, 25

West, Absalom Madden: buys house from Judge Clapp, 60; Civil War career, 60; death, 60; nomination to vice-presidency, 60; rebuilds Mississippi Central Railroad, 60

Wharton, Thomas Kelah: builds Airliewood, 113; builds Cedarhurst, 107

White Arches, *119, 126*; built by Jeptha V. Harris, 125; description, 125; subsequent owners, 125

Wilkinson, James, 4

William Johnson House, as part of Natchez National Historical Park, 40

Willis, Henry, obtains land grant for site of Rosalie, 15

Willis, Joseph: architect for Madison County Courthouse, 24; as architect for Mississippi State Lunatic Asylum, 24

Wilson, Andrew: buys Rosalie, 16; flees to Texas during Civil War, 16

Wilson, Samuel: builds Wilson-Gilruth House, 35; death in duel, 35; Yazoo City businesses, 35

Wilson-Gilruth House, *34, 36*; built by Samuel Wilson, 35; during Civil War, 35; sold to I. N. Gilruth, 35; use as hospital, 35; use of pre-fabricated elements, 35

Windsor, xiii, xiv, 24, 26, 70

Wohlden, 82, *87, 88, 89*; built by David Fulton, 86; Civil War, 88; description, 86; description of gardens, 88; modernization, 89; subsequent owners, 88

Worthington, Elisha, 64

Worthington, Isaac, 64

Worthington, Samuel, 64; losses during Civil War, 6

Worthington, William, builds Belmont, 64

Young, George Hampton: builds Waverley, 123; business ventures, 120; death, 123; during Civil War, 123; moves to Mississippi, 120

Young, Lucy Woodson Watkins: dies before completion of Waverley, 120; moves to Mississippi, 120; plants boxwoods at Waverley, 120

Young, Valerius, inherits Waverley, 123

Young, William: death and abandonment of Waverley, 123; inherits Waverley, 123; gambling parties, 123